Fear of Fiction

11/22/91

SUNY Series in Modern Jewish Literature and Culture
Edited by Sarah Blacher Cohen

Fear of Fiction

*Narrative Strategies
in the Works of
Isaac Bashevis Singer*

DAVID NEAL MILLER

State University of New York Press
Albany

Previously published excerpts of *Fear of Fiction*:

a. Portions of Chapter 2 were published as "Fiction as Reportage: Recurrent Narrative Situations in the Works of Isaac Bashevis Singer," *The Germanic Review*, 58, 3 (Summer 1983), 106–14; editorial offices of *The Germanic Review* are located at Columbia University, 320 Hamilton Hall, New York, NY 10027.

b. Portions of Chapter 3 were published as "History as Fiction: Isaac Bashevis Singer's Pseudonymous Personas," *Colloquia Germanica*, I (1983), 45–55; editorial offices of *Colloquia Germanica* are located at The University of Kentucky, Department of Germanic Languages and Literatures, Lexington, KY 40506; editor: Professor Bernd Kratz.

c. Portions of Chapter 4 were published as "Isaac Bashevis Singer: The Interview as Fictional Genre," *Contemporary Literature*; editorial offices of *Contemporary Literature* are located at the University of Wisconsin, Department of English, Helen C. White Hall, 600 North Park Street, Madison, WI 53706.

Published by
State University of New York Press, Albany

© 1985 State University of New York

For information, address State University of New York Press,
State University Plaza, Albany, New York 12246

Library of Congress Cataloging in Publication Data

Miller, David Neal
    Fear of fiction.

    (SUNY series in modern Jewish literature and culture)
    Bibliography: p. 155
    1. Singer, Isaac Bashevis, 1904–   – Criticism
and interpretation.   I. Title.   II. Series.
PJ5129.S49Z82   1985   839'.0933   84-16448
ISBN 0-88706-009-9
ISBN 0-88706-010-2 (pbk.)

10   9   8   7   6   5   4   3   2   1

For Murray
and the others

Contents

Preface

Opening gambits in academic studies of Yiddish literary texts are, of necessity, a bit odd and untested – and all the more so when these texts are by a major author. Whereas the scholar of, say, Proust or Thomas Mann or Faulkner has an all-but-impassible mountain of critical writings to wend his or her way through, the scholar of Yiddish literature faces, as a rule, a critical tabula rasa. There are, to be sure, exceptions, but these are few. One thinks of – perhaps longs for – the heady days after the December Revolution when faculties of Yiddish and, indeed, independent research institutes devoted to the study of Yiddish literature were established in Minsk and Kiev, and of the important, if occasionally tendentious, scholarship produced by members of these institutes[1] before they (both members and institutes) were swept away in one or another of Stalin's purges. One thinks, too, of the projects undertaken by the philological sections of the Yidisher visnshaftlekher institut (YIVO) in interbellum Vilna, Warsaw, and New York.[2] For the most part, though, Yiddish literature – even in the period of its remarkable efflorescence in the early decades of this century[3] – was produced, distributed, read, and discussed in the near-absence of formal academic notice.[4]

Isaac Bashevis Singer would seem to have escaped the fate of his fellow-authors in Yiddish. While he made his mark too late to have been noticed by European literary scholars,[5] he has – at least since having come to the attention of an English readership through Saul Bellow's 1953 translation of "Gimpl tam" [Gimpl the Fool] for the *Partisan Review*[6] – been the subject of some half-dozen books,[7] scores of articles,[8] and a not inconsiderable number of doctoral dissertations.[9] Yet, with the exception of a very few articles (and of no books or dissertations), Singer's works have been examined only as he has culled and modified them for an anglophone audience – that is, in translations which are rarely as faithful to the originals as was Bellow's,[10] and from an exceedingly circumscribed corpus of translated texts. Indeed, few of Singer's translators even know Yiddish; they work, as a rule, from Singer's verbal ad hoc translations. Moreover, of the nearly nine hundred works published by Singer during the first quarter-century of his creative career,[11] fewer than ten have been translated; the untranslated corpus includes scores of short stories and some dozen novels, in addition to what must now be approaching five thousand pieces (memoirs, essays, book reviews, and works of less readily identifiable genre) published in the periodical press. One might argue – Buchen and Malin do, if somewhat circumspectly,[12] and Edward Alexander does with an admirable awareness of both the advantages and the limitations of such an approach[13] – that this English-language Singer is an author quite discrete from his Yiddish-language analogue; such a position is not without some theoretical justification, as long as one knows precisely what one is attempting to justify. Insofar as Singer's translated texts are taken as original texts (albeit of corporate authorship, considering the role of the translator), well and good; but insofar as statements about a particular translated text are taken as applying to the underlying Yiddish original, or – even more recklessly – statements about the corpus of translated texts are taken as applying to the corpus of underlying Yiddish originals, they are insupportable.

Whatever the justification of considering Singer an English-language author, I have proceeded from the assumption that his works are best considered as Yiddish texts and within a primarily Yiddish frame of reference. This, in turn, informs a number of my working methods. First I have tended to give more attention to the untranslated than to the translated canon; it has not been as much a matter of bringing unknown works to light (though this does provide a measure of satisfaction) as of selecting texts for discussion without reference to their availability in translation: bibliographical arithmetic accounts for the ultimate ratio of untranslated to translated texts. Second, I have chosen as primary focus texts of a specific cast – those which show a marked degree of generic mixing, especially where that mixing juxtaposes conventionally fictive and non-fictive elements in a single text. Third, I have decided not to stray from Singer's works to broader questions of Singer's place in the eight hundred-year tradition of literature in Yiddish, in the self-consciously modernist Yiddish tradition of which he is a reluctant member, or in the broader tradition of Western literature in other languages. Although occasional allusions to works by other authors has proven useful or necessary, I have, as a rule, thought it best to keep my gaze fixed firmly on Singer's large, and largely-unexplored, body of works.

By so doing, a number of promising avenues of investigation were, a priori, left untravelled. Singer's mixing of fictional and non-fictional elements invites further examination in a broader context; works as diverse as J. P. Hebel's *Kalendargeschichten* and modern works of "faction" come to mind,[14] as do the various *mayse* subgenres of Yiddish folk literature which claim literal historicity for obvious fictions. ("Der rebe vos iz gevorn a vervolf" [The Rabbi Who Became a Werewolf], for example, begins with the redundant if formulaic "Dos iz an emese mayse-shehoye" [This is a true story].)[15] But all this lies beyond the scope of the present study. Fortunately, the foundations of a comparative view of Singer's accomplishments are currently being made by others – by Kazin and Baumgarten on Singer's relation to nineteenth-century America fiction,[16] by Shmeruk on Singer's relation to the Polish literary scene,[17] by Slotnick and Wolitz on Singer's relation to major texts within the Yiddish literary tradition,[18] by Grossman on Singer and the conventions of literary autobiography.[19] These studies complement my own more narrowly-focused discussions of the blurring of distinctions between fiction and reportage in Singer's oeuvre. Breadth and depth are both desiderata.

Singer's works have not hitherto been systematically enumerated, and my *Bibliography of Isaac Bashevis Singer, 1924–1949* has been a happy by-product of the research invested in this study. Nor have Singer's works been adequately collected, even in the original Yiddish; this has necessitated recourse to periodical backfiles here and abroad and, in the notes, reference to sources not readily accessible. Wherever possible, however,

I refer the reader to the most accessible printing or reprinting — from which I also cite. These citations are given first in their original Yiddish, transcribed in accordance with the system promulgated by YIVO Institute for Jewish Research and adopted by the Library of Congress, the *MLA International Bibliography*, and the responsible scholarly community; these are followed by my own translations into accurate, if not always felicitous, English. Where published English translations are available, they are indicated in the notes; such translations should be used with caution, however, for the reasons indicated above.

I am grateful to a number of colleagues, without whose assistance this study would have been far longer in the offing. These include Dina Abramowicz (Librarian, YIVO Institute for Jewish Research), Zachary Baker (Yiddica Librarian, Jewish Public Library of Montreal), Murray Baumgarten (University of California, Santa Cruz), John Ellis (University of California, Santa Cruz), Miriam Flock (Stanford University), Anita Susan Grossman (Berkeley, California), Elias Schulman (Queens College, CUNY), Sara Schyfter (SUNY at Albany), Chone Shmeruk (Hebrew University of Jerusalem), Seth L. Wolitz (University of Texas at Austin), and Amnon Zipin (Judaica Librarian, The Ohio State University). I am indebted to editor Sarah Blacher Cohen for her exacting standards and good taste.

Thanks are also due my colleagues and students at The Ohio State University; to the Department of Judaic and Near Eastern Languages and Literatures, Frederic J. Cadora, Chairman; to the Melton Center for Jewish Studies, Yehiel Hayon, Director; and to the College of Humanities, G. Micheal Riley, Dean.

Chapter 1

Fiction as Reportage, I: Examples from the Early Works

*Poets make themselves free by their
stance towards earlier poets.*[1]

"The freedom to have a meaning of one's own," argues Harold
Bloom, "is wholly illusory unless it is achieved against a prior
plenitude of meaning which is tradition."[2] Though Singer is consistently reluctant to acknowledge a debt to any tradition—
especially an exclusively Yiddish one[3]—less guarded remarks in
untranslated and uncollected memoiristic pieces originally
published in the *Forverts* belie the disclaimers reiterated in his
English-language interviews. In his "Figurn un epizodn fun
literarishn fareyn" [Figures and Episodes from the Writers' Union],
for example, Singer mentions how, even as a young man in
Bilgoray, he read randomly but voraciously in those secular
literary works which found their way to the isolated Galician
shtetl; his reading included most major authors of the classical
and post-classical generations: Y.-Y. Linetski, Sh.-Y. Abramovitsh,
Sh. Rabinovitsh, Y.-L. Perets, Dovid Frishman, H.-D. Nomberg,
Avrom Reyzen, Dovid Bergelson, Pinkhes Kaganovitsh, and
others:

> Yedes bukh iz geven far mir a gesheenish. Yeder zhurnal oder
> tsaytung vos hot zikh farvalgert keyn Bilgoray iz geven far mir
> an antdekung. Di ale mekhabrim zenen in a zin geven mayne
> kroyvim un ikh hob gehat mit zey kheshboynes.

1

[Each Yiddish book was for an event. ... Each journal or newspaper that turned up in Bilgoray was for me a discovery. All the authors were, to a certain degree, my relatives and I had to settle some scores with them.][4]

A discussion of each of these scores settled would lead unacceptably, though not unpleasantly, far afield, but we should note at the outset that the invocation and manipulation of literary tradition was Singer's earliest consistent narrative strategy.[5]

Before examining Singer's manipulation of the tradition he inherited as a young writer in interbellum Poland, we must establish what, precisely, that tradition consisted of for him. First, there *was* a tradition, rather than simply a corpus of texts. Moreover, there was a general awareness that such a tradition existed. This would not have been the case a half-century earlier, when Sholom Aleichem set out to posit and popularize the notion of a "zhargonishe literatur" [vernacular literature] with a history and qualitative authorial hierarchy. As Dan Miron persuasively documents,[6] Sholom Aleichem thought it necessary to invent the fiction of a Yiddish literary tradition in order to provide writers with normative models then lacking; some forty-five years later, the Yiddish avant-garde in its many groupings and regroupings were issuing manifestos announcing the Yiddish writers' autoemancipation from a tradition already perceived of as ossified and oppressive. Singer pointedly distances himself from the avant-garde's program of creation ex nihilo: for him, literary tradition and the conventions it had engendered were too valuable as foils against which to write texts which undermine that very tradition.

There had been fewer than a dozen Yiddish-language periodicals appearing in the entire world when Sholom Aleichem began publishing his *Folksbiblyotek* in 1888. Even then however, the Yiddish press had a voracious appetite for *reportazhn*, feuilletons, and other short pieces. Yiddish literary production in America patterned itself on the most prestigious of Anglo-American organs – the journal and little magazine. But whereas these favored by format the short story and, to a lesser extent, the novella, both prestige and opportunity favored the far shorter piece in Europe. There were several reasons for this. First, the feuilleton was a respected genre with stable features in both Central and Eastern Europe. Second, in interbellum Poland alone, more than 33 Yiddish dailies, 93 weeklies, and over 100 periodicals of general and cultural orientation were appearing in 1938-39.[7] The great majority of these—journals and newspapers alike—were measured not in words or pages, but in columns above or below the fold. (This was the case even with the *Literarishe bleter,* Poland's most prestigious literary magazine and the place of Singer's initial employ.)

Thus while Sholom Aleichem had to invent the fiction of a Yiddish literary tradition, Singer had to wade through conflicting claims of several traditions and more than a few avant-garde movements (e.g. the *Khalyastre* and *Albatros* groupings in Eastern Europe and the *inzikhistn* [introspectivists] in New York). Clearly, then, there had to be some selectivity in the mastery of traditions as fluid and diverse as those Singer found in 1925, the date of his first published appearance; he surely could not have come to terms with them all. In general, Singer ignored not only the avant-garde, but—more interestingly, perhaps—also the persistent if no longer pervasive monologue forms pioneered by Sholom Aleichem; indeed, Singer avoided writing in the first person until early 1943.[8]

Withal, it would be mistaken to view Singer's early canon as standing outside the mainstream of Yiddish literary production: to do so would be to fall prey both to Singer's later claim of autotelicity and to the notion of a literary tradition defined by American scholars with their own cultural program and frame of reference determined more by the Anglo-American than by the Yiddish literary landscape. History has been unkind to those literary genres and tendencies fostered by the tabloid format, once broadly popular and, to some degree, normative. Some of these tendencies had fixed generic tags, others were simply the aggregate of expectations characterizing those works which were, or which were considered, exemplary. I shall examine in turn two closely-related genres—the work of minimalist fiction and the *reportazh,* both in texts which preceded Singer's literary debut and in Singer's early, allusive, but ultimately subversive reworkings of generic norms.

I

The primary exponent – in some ways the inventor – of the minimalist fictional genre was Avrom Reyzen, characterized by Irving Howe in a discussion as informative in its inaccuracies as in its insights:

> Reisen [was a] wonderfully lovable figure – one would say "Franciscan" were not Reisen the quintessence of ethical *Yiddishkeit*. In his hundreds of little stories, Reisen has provided one of the truest portraits of Jewish life in Eastern Europe, and to a lesser extent of immigrant life in America. . . . Focusing upon familiar situations – a cantor has lost his voice, a poor householder cannot pay rabbinical tuition for his son – Reisen wrote in a manner that reminds one of those designers who by manipulating of few sticks create the illusion that a bare stage is Lear's palace. . . . So thoroughly was Reisen at home in his culture, so free of any wish to move back to a Hebraic milieu or forward to a cosmopolitan one, he could write as if to be explicit were an indelicacy.[9]

Howe correctly characterizes Reyzen's sensibilities, but he might better have located his stories' character in their formal qualities, especially considering that Howe describes a broadly popular genre, rather than the corpus of a single author, albeit its most distinguished practitioner. Reyzen's stories are not entirely plotless; it is only that their story (borrowing E. M. Foster's distinction between "plot" and "story")[10] typically begins near the denouement – that is, after all possibility of effective action has passed. In "Di oreme kehile" [The Poor (Jewish) Community].[11] for example, a mild act of communal profligacy – the engaging of a travelling cantor and his choir to lead a Sabbath service – has so depleted the town's coffers that it cannot afford a prayer leader for High Holy Days' services. Fallback plans are discussed but rejected, which does not prevent the townspeople from suggesting ameliorative plans they know in advance to be impossible: wealthier householders cannot put up money, since there are none; the *bal-tekie* [shofar blower], an impoverished student, cannot be begrudged the three rubles he stands to earn for working in the neighboring village – besides, the shofar is itself in hopeless disrepair. In effect, the story was over before narration commenced.

Reyzen does not suppress plot to foreground character, however. Little background data is ever offered on the stories' characters; they are defined by and limited to their function in Reyzen's near-plots. The narration, customarily in the third person by an anonymous and uncharacterized narrator, is curiously circumscribed: occasional information is given about the events preceding or following the framed fable time, but the narrator rarely claims access to his character's thoughts. Nor, finally, could the restricted length of the minimalist fiction sustain much in the way of character analysis, even if such was desired.

With both plot and character reduced to minimum, only the narrative consciousness remains. And this consciousness is remarkably consistent from piece to piece, permitting a gradual unfolding of the narrator's consciousness and concerns. The narration is self-conscious and draws attention to itself. Passages of nature description in heightened prose – a profligate expenditure of *Erzaehlzeit* in so short a narrative – comment not as much on the stories' thin plots as on the narrative consciousness. Moreover, this presence is an intertextual constant.

The net result is works of diminished fictiveness: the narrator's distance and lack of omniscience, as well as his reappearance in texts as their only common element, make these pieces resemble the bylined prose commentary – a nonfictional genre with claims to literal historicity. It is to this narrative situation which Howe was probably reacting when he asserts that "Reisen had provided one of the truest portraits of Jewish life." Reyzen's fictional nets, however, were certainly cast no wider than those of, say, Perets, Ash, or Bergelson, and they were nowhere cast very deep: these stories seem of especial value as recorded history only because their narrative strategies sustain that claim.

It is understandable and, with retrospective logic, nearly inevitable that Singer should have chosen this narrative mode, of which Reyzen was the most popular exponent. First, it stands on the border of fiction and reportage – important for an author who had yet fully to prepare himself to subvert the expectations engendered by less ambiguously fictive genres. Second, Singer's minimalist fictions appeared in the periodical (usually tabloid) press, as had Reyzen's before them. His readers were thus predisposed to respond appropriately to the pieces' common formal elements in their shared context. Third, Reyzen's frequent

mawkishness fairly invites deflation: his narrators are unrestrained in their sympathy for unhappy characters and, with
anthropomorphizing zeal, also with "unhappy" inanimate objects
(a deserted synagogue, a violated coin bank). Singer's narrators,
for their part, display strict reportorial neutrality, despite their
depiction of far greater suffering (a consumptive child, a paralyzed
young wife, a suicidal rabbi). Withal, generic parallels are
unmistakable.

A single, early story, "Eyniklekh" [Grandchildren], is typical.[12]
The word is negatively marked in hassidic usage: it refers to the
inevitable reassertion of genetic and Malthusian determinants in
a rabbinical line of descent beginning with a single *rebe*
[charismatic leader]. All offspring cannot inherit the originator's
qualities, nor could Jewish society absorb a geometric increase
of *rabeyim*; inevitably, lines go into decline, creating a class of
impoverished *rabeyim* with tiny followings. Singer's narrator
depicts with a lyricism ironically reminiscent of Reyzen's the court
of one Sender Leyvi Karver, a grandson of the famous Belzer *rebe*,
where he drunkenly presides over the few women who bring him
occasional offerings of food and over his son, a eunuch by birth.
Unlike Thomas Mann's *Buddenbrooks*, which Singer early read
and admired,[13] this *Verfall einer Familie* provides no occasion for
reflection. Indeed, the rabbi had all but stopped speaking before
the story's beginning, and the narrative frame provides no access to his thoughts. Nor are those rare thoughts he does express
very coherent: he spends quite some time, for example, wondering whether he had ever had a daughter called Dinele, and
whether he should lament her death. Eventually, and offstage,
he kills himself, though the story ebbs for some 250 words after
the death is discovered. As with Reyzen, nature depictions in
heightened prose often substitute for plot and character
development:

S'iz gevorn tunkl, der himl hot zikh farvolknt vi tsum regenen,
di matseyves zenen gevorn modne shtil, ongelodn, vi in dervar-
tung, un grel-vays. . . . Etlekhe getseylte kroen, groyse un shvere,
zenen gefloygn fun boym tsum boym, getsaplt mit di fligl, ale mol
a fal getun arop un derbay a shtiln krake getun.
[It grew dark; the sky clouded over as if to rain; the gravestones
became strangely white. . . . A number of crows, large and heavy,

flew from tree to tree, flapped their wings jerkily, dropped downward each time and let out a quiet caw while falling.][14]

Though Reyzen's sensibilities are being mocked, his narrative situation receives the praise of imitation. Here too, plot and character are suppressed, and the reportorial consciousness is, by default and design, foregrounded. "Eyniklekh" thus demonstrates Singer's exploitation of the minimalist genre to further the blurring of distinctions between fiction and reportage.

The narrative consciousness, as in Reyzen, dominates the narrative, drawing more attention to itself than to its narrative material. Though anonymous, the narrator often functions as character: he has quirks of craft and what might best be described as narrative tics. Reyzen's narrator is fond of anthropomorphic simile; Singer's prefers lengthy one-sentence paragraphs of facial description which are often the only characterizing devices he permits himself:

> Tsurikgekumen . . . iz er mit vayse hor un der shvartser tsuprine, mit a harter lang-nisht-razirter bershtldiker bord arum di ayngefalene bakn, a hoykher, an oysgedarter, mit a lang-gevorene[r] mrukevater noz un mit tsvey boylet-aroysgezetste, tunkele oygn, vos zeyere galkes kukn akegn zikh shtolern-kalt un shvaygndik, mit fartsoygene bremen fun ineveynikster akshones, on kheyshek optsugebn emetsn din-vekheshbn un tsu tselozn zikh mit mayses.
> [He returned with white hair and his black forelock, with a tough, long-unshaven bristly beard about his sunken cheeks, tall, haggard, with a peevish nose that had grown long and with two bulding dark eyes whose eyeballs stared at one another steely-cold and without desire to account for himself to anybody and to let loose with stories.][15]

The syntax here recalls the heightened prose of both Singer and Reyzen's nature descriptions, while the striking similarities among Singer's facial descriptions also serve to foreground the narrative consciousness. Compare the following description to the one previously cited:

> Reb Sender Leyvi Karver [iz geven] a hoykher, di peyses oysgekrokhn, mit a langer, gedikhter, fartabakter bord, mit lange

vontses, mit gedikhte bremen vi bershtlekh, mit a langer,
mrukevater noz, vos is aroptsutsu broyn-bloy gevezn un mit
groyse, royte, broygeze mit blut-farlofene oygn.
[Reb Sender Leyvi Karver (was) tall, his sidelocks fallen out, with
a long, thick, tabacco-stained beard, with a long mustache, with
thick brows like bristles, with a long peevish nose which was
turned downward (and) brownish-blue and with large, red, angry
bloodshot eyes.][16]

These similarities serve both to bind Singer's minimalist fictions to one another and to set them off against those of the genre's
foremost practitioner. These countertexts are not as subversive
of the generic norms of minimalist fiction as his later works would
be of the norms of other established genres: at the outset it was
nearly enough that he claimed a dominant genre as his own. Yet,
for all, that structural and narrative norms were hardly violated,
Singer's *Auseinandersetzung* with Reyzen's gentler pieces could
hardly have been more pronounced in terms of tone and sensibility. Reyzen's narrator compensates, or attempts to compensate, for the plotlessness of his fictions by pleasantly lyric nature
descriptions; in the same vein, he attempts to enliven entropic
society by engaged narrative interventions which redirect attention from the narrated to the narrating consciousness. Finally,
his repeated use of anthropomorphic simile animates objects
wherever his characters have lost the will or ability to act. In the
end, Reyzen undercuts the bleakness of his vision by the geniality
of its depiction.

For his part, Singer has his narrators augment, rather than
ameliorate, the despair and deadness of their material: lyric inter-
ludes dwell not on ripening fields of grain but, rather, on car-
rion birds and peevish noses. That these are described in the
heightened prose Reyzen reserves for his most lyrically life-
affirming interpolations is surely a recasting – immodest in intent
if modest in scope – of the norms of minimalist fiction. Singer
was not long to remain as unambitious.

II

Singer also mastered a concurrent genre, related to but
discrete from minimalist fiction: the *reportazh*. Here the matter

of generic tagging is a bit less settled than with the more mature genres. A work might equally be labelled *reportazh* [piece of reportorial writing], *portret* [portrait], *bild* [picture, portrait], *vinyet(ke)* [vignette], *minyatur* [miniature].[17] If the nomenclature is a bit unstable, the generic norms are clear enough:

(a) the narrative situation is generally limited to a single place (e.g. a room) or a single occasion (e.g. a walk, a dinner party);

(b) there is an extensive description of surroundings;

(c) the reported incident is, in fictional terms, only randomly gleaned (e.g. from passers-by, or from passing among a shifting cast of colloquants);

(d) an objective basis of focus of the narrator's attention is, accordingly, lacking;

(e) to the parataxis of reported incident is frequently added an inconclusiveness of denouement;

(f) the narrative consciousness is restricted to recording externals, and is rarely granted even limited omniscience;

(g) there is a marked foregrounding of the linguistic surface;

(h) the narrative voice not only draws attention to itself but, as the story's central focus and sole unifying strand, feels at liberty to provide transitions solely by personal association – thus satisfying a residual need for an ordering principle while establishing itself as character.

Here there is no single author who can stand for all of his colleagues. Nonetheless, it is – somewhat paradoxically, perhaps – quite a bit easier to enumerate the generic norms of the *reportazh* than those of minimalist short fiction. For, while exceptions to the earlier generalizations exist, even within the corpus of Reyzen's own work, the *reportazh* was a remarkably stable genre; one author's works differed from another's more in matters of personal sensibility than in those of form and narrative prerogatives.[18] For convenience, we shall look at a single *reportazh* by an important, if nearly forgotten, master of the genre – Perets Opotshinski.

Opotshinski (1895 - 1942 or 1943), a writer as gentle as Reyzen and one a good deal more self-effacing, was a regular writer for *Undzer ekspres* [Our Express].[19] This was a major afternoon daily in interbellum Warsaw; like, say, *PM*, *Undzer ekspres* emphasized

commentary, rather than hard news, and like the Hearst afternoon papers, tended at times toward a rather lurid sensationalism.

"In Krashinskis gortn" [In Kraszinski Gardens], undated in
Opotshinski's *Gezamlte shriftn* [Collected Writings], was almost
certainly published in *Undzer ekspres* in the late 1920's or early
1930's.[20] It is even shorter than the Reyzen pieces—approximately
450 words. As in "Di oreme kehile" [The Poor Community], the
narrator's presence is immediately felt; here, however, the narration is in the first person singular. The piece is a reportazh
recording the narrator's impressions of a walk through a public
park, punctuated by snatches of overheard dialogue. Interestingly,
the landscape elements are only briefly-glimpsed backdrops for
the human ones; two descriptive paragraphs in heightened prose
serve more to establish the narrator as a controlling sensibility
than to tell about their ostensible subjects. Sandwiched between
descriptions of bench sitters immobilized by the heat and by their
inability to find work is the first of the nature descriptions:

> Der vaser-shpigl funem taykhl hot a matovn, fetn, grinbroynlekhn
> opglants, un di shvanen shvimen iber im mit farshlofene,
> aropgelozte kep. [The surface of the stream catches an opaque,
> green-bluish reflection, and the swans swim over it with sleepy,
> bowed heads.] (p. 154)

The narrative perspective shifts rapidly, a correlative of the narrators's physical passage through the park and of his transient
perceptions; the tense, as we have seen, is invariably the present.
At times, the narrative voice disappears entirely and yields to
the voices of those whom it passes:

> −"Un vos tut der man?"
> −"Vos zol er ton? Er handlt oykh in gas; loyft arum a gantsn tog,
> ober keyn parnose iz fun dem alem nito."
> ["What's your husband doing?"
> "What should he be doing? He's also doing business in the streets,
> running around all day long, but not earning a living from it all."]
> (p. 155)

At other times, individuals merge (as the day itself merges into
dusk), and the narrator presents the feelings of the collective:

Der ovnt falt tsu . . . Kinder veynen in di vegelekh. Di mames,
vos zitsn dernebn oyf mitgebrakhte kleyne benkelekh, shoklen
zey tsu un bamien zikh zey ayntsushlefern, velndik in der tunkl-
sho khotsh opruen a bisl. S'dukht zikh: ot-ot, nokh a bisl, veln di
ovnt-shoen brengen di derleyzung.
[Evening falls . . . Babies cry in their carriages. Their mothers, sitting beside them on small benches they'd brought along, rock them
and try to make them sleepy, wanting themselves to rest a bit in
the dusk. They think: soon, soon, in just a little while, the evening will bring release.] (p. 156)

Apparently, the thoughts of the collective are more accessible to
the narrator than are those of individuals, and thus he speaks
for, as much as to, them. It would, however, be an error to view
this as genuine omniscience; it is, more likely, a token of the narrator's difficulty in maintaining his critical distance from the
people he is describing – people very much like himself. In fact,
by the final paragraphs of "In Krashinskis gortn," the narrator
becomes himself a character described in the third person – a telling, if stylistically confusing, collapse of narrative distance:

Eyner iz avekgegengen un der oylem tserukt zikh. Lebn mir zitst
a froy in di yorn. . . . Zi batrakht a vayle ir nayem shokhn –
m i kh heyst es – un git mir a freg, vi shpet es iz. [Someone got
up and the people adjust themselves (on the bench). Next to me
sits a woman of a certain age. . . . For a while, she examines her
new neighbor – that is to say, *me* – and asks me the time.]
(p. 156)

The *reportazh* does not as much end as stop. To be sure, the
onset of evening provides a sense of closure of sorts, but this is
undercut in several ways. First, the conversations are paratactic
and inconclusive. Second, evening brings yet more persons to the
park – more persons to be described, overheard, and commented
upon; we leave the narrator still sitting on a bench. Third, evening brings an intensification of the natural oppressiveness –
a constricture, rather than an opening out. Even the sentence
structure, earlier so carefully crafted, collapses: "Es iz eng.
Dushne. Der gortn otemt shver. . ."[It is crowded. Stuffy. The
garden breathes heavily . . .] (p. 158, Opotshinski's elipses). The
only closure is, finally, a waning of narrative energy.

"Sale," published by Singer in the *Literarishe bleter* for January 1932,[21] announces itself as a portrait of an individual – as common an object of *reportazh* as Opotshinski's group of people in Kraszinski Gardens. What is unusual, however, is that Sale is not even mentioned until nearly halfway into the piece, and that she first appears at the end of the second of three columns. What one does have, without preliminaries, is a meticulously detailed description of a number of artifacts in "di dire vu Sale iz oyfgehodevet gevorn" [the apartment where Sale was raised]. In itself, this approach has historical sanction: one thinks of Balzac's descriptions of easy chairs and room decorations. The decorations in Sale's family's living room are precisely, if unappetizingly catalogued:

> Iber di vent – tsetumpete oysneyekhtser, fun oplakirter vlitshke, bapintlte mit flign-tsoye. . . . S'hengt do – Moyshe rabeynu mit yungerish-royte bekelekh un mit tsvey fledervishn oyf beyde zaytn shtern, Napoleon oyfn ferd, groyse arumgeremte fotografyes fun tsevaksene bobes in tife sheytlen un zeydes mit tsugeplatshte sametene kaplen oyf di lomdishe kep un mit gvirish-karbirte berd. [All over the walls – frayed embroideries covered with shellac and speckled with fly droppings. . . . Hanging here is a Moses with youthfully red cheeks and with two feather dusters on either side of his forehead; Napoleon on horseback; large framed photographs of overample grandmothers in full wigs and grandfathers with flattened velvet caps on their learned heads and with the curled beards of the wealthy.] (p. 7)

We note at the outset two devices by means of which the narator reveals himself as mediating intellect: first, he is presumably located within the room he describes ("Hanging here . . ."); second, he makes use of marked affixes in a personal aesthetic evaluation of the wall hangings. An *oysneyekhts* is not merely "something embroidered," for example, but "something poorly/repulsively embroidered"; *tsevaksn* is not as much "ample" as "overgrown."

These attitudes are not, however, situationally motivated; that is, they reflect neither on the occasion of the *reportazh* nor on the role of Sale's surroundings on the piece's central action. For one thing, an occasion is entirely lacking; one does not know, despite the narrator's unimpeded view of the living room, precisely where he is situated. He is not, to be sure, the omniscient third-person narrator of traditional fiction, but, rather, the observing intelligence of the *reportazh*. On the other hand, neither statement nor clue permits the reader quite to naturalize him as character. Like Virginia Woolf's narrator in "The Shooting Party,"[22] Singer's narrator shares the limitations of the narrative's other characters without, however, taking up any space. The narrator here lacks even the pretext of a walk past the characters whose reported speech and actions constitute the entirety of Opotshinski's *reportazh*. Singer retains, then, the formal narrative structure of the *reportazh* without its conventional – or, indeed, any – motivation.

The same may be said of the sequence of observations in a *reportazh*, which is, as a rule, dependent upon two factors – the narrator's changing physical relationship to the objects and persons described, and the associations they evoke in his otherwise inaccessible consciousness. Thus external, "objective" determinants limit the free play of the narrator's imagination while personal and idiosyncratic factors invest certain of those externals with greater emotional weight – and hence *Erzaehlzeit* – than their role in the passing scene would ordinarily warrant. One factor holds the other in check.

The spatial indeterminancy of Singer's narrator does not, at the outset, appear to affect the other conventions of the *reportazh*. Thus, for example mention of Napoleon astride his horse leads the narrator to describe Sale's father astride his easy chair. As in Opotshinski's randomly-gleaned conversations, the father is caught in mid-declamation:

> [Der tate] dertseylt komivoyazhorishe khokhmes, papet bilike papiroslekh in vinkl moyl, hust, shpayt in nozfartshaylekhl un taynet: –Yidn, s'iz khoyzek . . . s'et do gornisht vern! . . . [(Her father) tells travelling salesmen's witticisms, sticks cheap cigarettes in the corner of his mouth, coughs, spits into his handkercheif and complains: "Jews, it's ridiculous. . . Nothing will come of it! . . ."] (p. 7)

Attention to Sale's father brings Sale's mother to mind, and the narrator interrupts his survey of the room to quote – again in mid-conversation – her words to an unidentified gentleman caller:

[Di mame] taynet, zislekh-opnarerish un mit a ful moyl drobne-
arayngemakhte tseyndlekh: – bite, zitsn zi . . . Sale kumt bald
arayn . . . Kukn zi dervayl durkh dem album . . . [(Her mother)
complains with syrupy coquettishness and a mouth full of dainty
false teeth: "Please be seated. . . . Sale's coming soon. . . . In the
meantime, look through this album. . . ."] (p. 7, Singer's ellipses)

Neither quotation is in itself remarkable, but their juxtaposition in what one assumes to be simultaneous colloquy creates
a grotesquely *Bald Soprano*-like effect – animated speaking with,
apparently, nobody listening. In an attempt to make more sense
of these goings-on, the reader might like to reconsider the data
given about father and mother as representing typical attitudes
and utterances, rather than actions and speech acts in the narrative present. The tense, compound past throughout, offers little
enough guidance: Yiddish lacks an imperfect, and the
pluperfect – later to become a touchstone of Singer's prose style – is
rare. Use of the compound past may, then, indicate either the
narrative present or characteristic actions in the narrative past.
But to so read this scene would be to bracket out the only action
in nearly two-thirds of the *reportazh*; moreover, questioning the
time frame of the reported dialogue would, inevitably, lead to
questioning the parents' physical presence in the living room. This
in turn, would leave the reader with characters as elusive as the
narrator.

In what is perhaps the piece's only unassailable action, Sale
enters the room. She speaks with no one, however, nor does she
do anything once in the room. The remaining third of the *reportazh* purports to record her recent experience as a star-struck
would-be actress seeking the smallest of bit parts – on the casting
couch of a coarse and coarsely-Polonized Jewish film producer,
and at the artists' and writers' parties which she regularly attends.
Yet, like Wama in Ring Lardner's *"Clemo Uti* (The Water Lillies),"
who "enters from an exclusive waffle parlor [and] exits as if she
had had waffles,"[23] Sale evokes the narrator's lengthy and complex speculations merely by entering. The narrator carefully
avoids both conventional claims of omniscience, on the one hand,
and self-depiction as a character who might have had occasion
to observe Sale outside of her living room, on the other. In the

end, she is temporally as indeterminate as her parents and spatially as insubstantial as the narrator.

The conclusion of Singer's *reportazh* recalls that of Opotshinski in its entropic inconclusiveness. A film producer is overheard (though one cannot be certain whether the incident "actually" takes place or whether Sale's appearance merely prompts the narrator to posit it as a possible conversation):

> −Kon zayn, mirn aykh nutsn . . . gants meglekh . . . der iker−
> geduld . . . *a sakh* geduld! . . . ["It's possible we'll use you . . . quite
> possible. . . . The main thing is to have patience, *a lot* of patience!]
> (p. 8)

While the narrator of "In Krashinskis gortn" was reluctant to provide situational closure for his *reportazh* − we leave him sitting on a park bench − the surroundings which were so meticulously described assume the burden of closure by bringing the day, and the piece, to an end. But, since the surroundings in "Sale" have been deprived of all physical and temporal substantiality, they can ony continue to disorient even the reader accustomed to the lax denouements of the *reportazh*. Nevertheless, conventional norms have nowhere been violated but only honored at their most extreme.

Thus early in his career Singer had − intuitively, it would seem − already derived his typical strategy of undermining inherited genres and the attendant expectations they engender not by ignoring the conventions, but by reducing them to their starkest form. This is, in fact, radical experimentalism in the guise of conventional, conservative practice.

III

We have noted two pervasive, though nearly independent tendencies in Singer's oeuvre through about 1932: the selection of genres on the margins of fictiveness (minimalist fiction, *reportazh*) and the undermining of generic expectations. Thus far, only the former has significantly contributed to the process which I have sought to record − namely, the blurring of distinctions between the fictive and the historical. In this regard, it is of importance that "Sale," for example, is a *reportazh*, but of less importance that is strains, though ultimately does not violate, generic norms. In "A zokn: A khronik" [An Old Man: A Chronicle],[24] written in late 1932, however, both tendencies collaborate in the creation of a text whose ontological status is at once under- and overdetermined; this generic instability leads to a text which makes simultaneous, if incomplete, claims to fictiveness, on the one hand, and literal historicity, on the other. In important ways, "A zokn" is Singer's first mature work, a fact the author recognized by including it, alone of the shorter pieces from his pre-emigration canon, in a collection of his works in English translation; in the "Acknowledgements" to *Gimpel the Fool and Other Stories* (1957), Singer even draws attention to the early origins of "A zokn": "These stories were written during the last ten years with the exception of 'The Old Man,' which appeared in 1933 in Warsaw.[25]

The subtitle offers little initial guidance in apprehending the text, since *khronik* [chronicle] is not a contemporary generic tag. To be sure, chronicle-like genres enjoyed renewed popularity in the early decades of this century; one thinks of works cast in the shape of *zekhroynes* [memoirs, reminiscences], *memaurn* [memoirs], and *pinkosim* [(communal) registers] – the latter, we may recall, the frame of Sholom Aleichem's celebrated fiction, "Der farkishefter shnayder" [The Enchanted Tailor].[26] But *khronik* evokes, in this reader at least, only associations with the travel chronicle, an association hardly sustained by the piece's initial paragraph:

> Ven di milkhome hot zikh ongehoybn iz Khayim-Sakher fun Krokhmalne-gas in Varshe geven a yid a nogid, gehat far yeder tokhter a toyznter nadn un grod gehaltn bay nemen a gresere voynung, s'zol zayn an ort far an eydem a bentoyre (Y51).
> [At the beginning of the Great War, Chaim Sacher of Krochmalna Street in Warsaw was a rich man. Having put aside dowries of a thousand rubles each for his daughters, he was about to rent a new apartment, large enough to include a Torah-studying son-in-law (E127).]

This is the beginning of a traditional short story and poses no particular difficulty for the reader, even within the context of Singer's early writings: though minimalist fictions dominated his output, Singer had by 1933 published a number of *der-tseylungen* [short stories] and *noveln* [novellas].[27] We might, however, note an unusual – at least for Singer – degree of chronological and socio-political specificity in "A zokn"; events within the fictional frame are reported in conjunction with extra-literary historical events, although there is little causal relation-ship between the two. The relationship is, rather, associative: much as events rush by too rapidly to be assimilated (Warsaw is occupied several times during the course of World War I, with attendant social dislocations), so, too, do the waxings and – especially – wanings of the Sachar family fortunes. Within five paragraphs, the two sons, wife, and two daughters of the character who one had presumed to be the protagonist die; toward the end of the fifth paragraph, Khayim-Sakher himself dies. The sole sur-vivor is a grandfather who was not even mentioned at the outset; by default, as it were, the *khronik* becomes his.

With the grandfather the sole focus of attention, narrative prerogatives undergo a transformation as radical as the reorienta-tion of protagonist which preceded it. Historical allusions dis-appear absolutely, as do nearly all allusions to a world outside the apartment, which, for the first time, is described in detail reminiscent of "Sale." Paralleling the closing-in of narrative perspective is a closing-in of narrative omniscience. But this, too, is accomplished through an uneasy juxtaposition of conventions belonging to different genres. On the one hand, the narrator has frequent recourse of narrated monologue (*erlebte Rede*), collapsing the distance between himself and the old man and permitting the reader direct, if somewhat mediated, access to the latter's thoughts. This obviates the need for omniscient narration – a mode generally inevitable in texts with a single, unloquacious character – and thus emphasizes the reportorial aspect of this sec-tion. At times, however, the narrator draws attention to himself in interpolated passages in heightened prose – the touchstone of minimalist fiction:

S'iz gevorn harbstik-kalt un oysgelaytert. Kegn tunklgelblekhn, metushtishn likht fun oysgeshterntn himl hot a tshate tsign mit shvaygndider hasmode gesheylt di kore fun holts, vos iz gelegn

in shulhoyf greyt oyf vinter. A sove hot geklogt mit a vayberish
kol, iz ale mol antshvign gevorn un ongehoybn fun s'nay, vi oyf
a tsore, vos lozt zikh nit fargesn. . . . (Y60).
[The autumnal night was clear and cold; against the dark yellow,
dull glow of the starry sky, a flock of goats, silently absorbed,
peeled bark from the wood that had been piled in the synagogue
courtyard for the winter. As though complaining of an unforget-
table sorrow, an owl lamented in a womanish voice, falling silent
and beginning again, over and over (E135).]

These cannot have been the old man's thoughts: by the time he
leaves the apartment, he is nearly incoherent;[28] rather, the narrator has asserted himself as an independent character.

But to what end? In the course of only eleven paragraphs,
the reader has been given an overabundance of generic clues:
he has, in turn and sometimes simultaneously, been invited to
consider the piece as short story, *reportazh*, and minimalist fiction; to regard the narrator as convention, mediating intellect,
and character; to attend to or ignore the historical frame; to locate
and identify the central character. There are, I believe, two ways
of accounting for Singer's game of guess-the-genre – one motivated
by factors within the fiction, the other by Singer's general
reticence to produce texts of anambiguously fictional cast. The
former, Singer asserts, lends authority to the latter.

In the last of these fifteen paragraphs, the old man decides
to risk a journey to the Galician town of Janow, home of the Turisk
hassidim, and the well-remembered home of his youth. Whether
the town still existed, and whether the Turisk hassidim still lived
there, was – the old man suggests – unknown and unknowable in
the chaos of wartime Europe. Moreover, by this time the narrator's perspective is at one with that of its 90-year-old protagonist;
chronology, as well as its external social referents, are confused
or imprecise. (Perhaps a telegram to Janow, or a visit to the proper embassy – the story does take place after all, in the capital
of an independent Poland newly at peace – might have settled the
matter. But this would never have occurred to the old man and
would, as I shall argue, have been at odds with Singer's narrative
strategy.) It is important to note that the old man's rejection of
urban life was moral as well as utilitarian; Jewish life had become
too layered-over with secular accretions, too far removed from

the geographical sources of its spiritual vitality – the hassidic town courts – to sustain its weight. Material poverty was but the reflection of spiritual poverty.

As easily as the narrator had jettisoned two generations of the Sacher family, the old man decides to jettison the cradle of that family in favor of his own place of origin. And this is the point of the narrator's earlier generic sleight-of-hand: no urban, sophisticated genre could contain Moyshe-Ber, since he was not of the world which had given rise to secular literature. To do his protagonist justice, the narrator realized after attempting and rejecting a succession of narrative modes, would entail recourse to an older mode untainted by the urban experience. With this realization, the first of two numbered sections closes; interestingly, one generic norm is retained – the section is the traditional three-column length; this despite the latitude afforded by *Globus*, a magazine-format journal of which Singer was co-editor.

The second section keeps the promise of the piece's subtitle: it is a chronicle of Moyshe-Ber's return to Janow. As such, it recalls a pan-European travel literature accumulated from the high middle ages until well into the eighteenth century. Individual works within this tradition make quite different claims to literal historicity (although *some* claim was generally mandated); a corpus containing Benjamin of Tudela's earnest and precise *Massoth Rabbi Benjamin* [Travels of Rabbi Benjamin] (1543)[29] also includes Christian Reuter's parodic *Schelmuffskys Wahrhafftige, Curioese und sehr gefaehrliche Reisebeschreibung zu Wasser und Lande* (1696).[30] But the travel chronicle inevitably lays mixed claim to literal historicity. On the one hand, its primary raison d'être is to acquaint geographically and ethnographically naive readers with foreign customs and lands. As such, its claims are to strict historicity. On the other hand, in a practice dating back at least to Herodotus, the travel chronicles also admitted interpolations of the most fantastic anecdotes and legends. By invoking the tradition of the travel account, then, Singer was placing his own text in apposition to a body of texts which themselves stood midway between fiction and reportage, drawing their authority from both.

The narrative stance in the travel chronicle is that of observer as outsider. Though the chronicle gains veracity in that its teller was actually present at the events chronicled (interpolated tales excluded), the observing intellect is, despite the travels it has undertaken, customarily no more sophisticated than that of his homebound readers. There is, accordingly, no attempt at imaginative leap or sympathetic contract withthe host societies — they exist as exotic grist for the chronicler's mill. This is one reason why so much data and incident can be included in relatively short volumes: with no attempt to penetrate the cultures they portray, exhaustion of their material, rather than mere wanderlust, is motivation for moving on. "A zokn" patterns its second part on the travel chronicle, recounting Reb Moyshe-Ber's return through foreign and hostile territory to the Turisk home of his youth. In the course of three short paragraphs, he has himself smuggled accross the Austrian border under a load of straw; falls ill with dysentery and is thrown into a poorhouse; discovers peasants wearing the ancient Ukranian tunics and tasseled quadrangular caps; is jailed by the militia but ransomed, months later, by the Jewish community of Zamość; lives on roots and berries wandering through strange forests; is beaten and has his boots stolen by a gang of shepherds. The narrator restricts himself to Moyshe-Ber's point of view throughout and, for his part, Moyshe-Ber describes his adventures with scrupulous eye for detail, but without any understanding of the motivation and behind the events and persons he describes. Gentiles encountered, for example, speak either *goyish* ["Gentile"] or *yoyvanish* ["Greek"]; it is important to record that they do not speak Yiddish or Polish (i.e. that they are foreign), but not to find out precisely what language they do speak.

Singer has, as we have seen, moved the generic locus of his text back a number of centuries, much as Moyshe-Ber moves back to an earlier — though by no means medieval — society. Yet, immediately prior to the old man's arrival in Janow, the text's allusiveness moves farther back still: there are unmistakable allusions to Jesus' parable of the return of the prodigal son (Luke 15:11-32). We remember that Jesus speaks of a young man who "took his journey into a far country and there wasted his substance with riotous living" (13). The situation changes for the worse and, after suffering near-starvation abroad, the son returns to beg his father's forgiveness and live as a hired servant.

But the father said to his servants, Bring forth the best robe and
put it on him, and put a ring on his hand, and shoes on his feet:
And bring hither the fatted calf, and kill it, and let us eat, and
be merry: For this my son was dead, and is alive again; he was
lost and is found. And they began to be merry (22-24).

Parallels in "A zokn" demand the reader's attention. Like the
prodigal son, Moyshe-Ber had left his hassidic family to live
abroad – Krokhmalna Street in Warsaw was both politically and
spirituually a foreign country. Initial good fortune ("riotous living")
was followed by near-starvation: "Der zokn [hot] gegesn um-
tsaytike kerner fun tvue" [He fed on unripened grain] (Y58, E155).
Compare this with Luke: "And he would fain have filled his belly
with the husks that the swine did eat: and no man gave unto him"
(16). Like the prodigal's brother, the first group of younger Turisk
hassidim were reluctant to welcome Moyshe-Ber back, but the
elders celebrated his return with gefilte fish and kreplekh, adequate stands-in for the fatted calf:

Der gantser oylem khsidim hot tsuzamen, vi der mineg iz,
getrunken bronfn un farbisn mit lekekh. M'hot teykef dem altn
derkent. S'iz gevorn a groyse simkhe, vayl m'hot im shoyn lang
gehaltn far a mes (Y61).
[(They) recognized the new arrival at once, and there was great
rejoicing for he had long been thought dead (E158).]

In this instance, Singer as implied author must assume that narrator's allusive tasks: this parable is presumably unknown to an
elderly Jew with traditional, if extensive, schooling, and to a narrative consciousness nearly identical to that of its protagonist.
By so doing, he makes Moyshe-Ber's decision to return all the
more plausible: the old man, it would seem, is involved in a process all the implications of which remain closed to him. Be that
as it may, the allusive locus is no longer medieval, but New
Testament.
     The process has not yet concluded, however, for Moyshe-Ber
suggests Biblical (i.e. Hebrew Scriptural) antecedents for his
biography. Whether Moyshe-Ber thought of himself as a new
Moyshe rabeynu who, after forty years abroad (he had left Janow

in his early fifties and returned in his early nineties), was permitted to enter the Promised Land we are not told, but he did think of himself as an Avrom avinu, fathering a child and beginning a line (his son and grandchildren having perished abroad) in his hundredth year:

> V'Avrom ben me'as shono – hot er ibergekhazert dem posek fun der toyre. – behivoled loy eys Yitskhok benoy. Vatoymer Sore taskhoyk oso li eloyhim kol hashoymeya yitsakhak li. Dem yingl hot er a nomen gegebn Yitskhok (Y 49).
> ["And Abraham was a hundred years old," he recited, "When his son Isaac was born unto him. And Sarah said: 'God hath made me laugh so that all who hear will laugh with me.'" He named the boy Isaac (E137).]

Moyshe-Ber has reached the end of his *neshome-ekspeditsye* by arriving at the point of origin. With this passage, Singer's narrator concludes his chronicle; indeed, he must conclude it here, for to regress any further would be to embed Moyshe-Ber's return in a pre- and hence non-Jewish text. And, the narrative structure of "A zokn" suggests, personal history – or at least this personal history – cannot be understood except with reference to those genres which are literary correlates of a particular stage in the protagonist's development.

What has Singer accomplished by burdening a rather simple story with this baggage of literary allusion? First, of course, there is the performance for its own sake; whatever the purpose, it is a remarkable tour de force for a still-fledgling writer to have written a twelve-page text which functions successivley as short story, *reportazh*, minimalist fiction, travel chronicle, New Testament parable and Hebrew Scriptural analogue. Second, there is the fact that each of the attempted genres itself stands midway between fiction and reportage: the *reportazh* and minimalist fiction are, as I have discussed, only mildly fictitious; the travel chronicle intermingles fact and fiction without admitting of a contradiction between the two; the Hebrew Scriptures, though hardly naturalistic, certainly claim literal historicity and are so regarded in orthodox circles; and even the parable would claim to be more universal – hence truthful – than the truth. Only the short story, as which the first five paragraphs are cast, is a conventioally fictive genre. Thus, while the texts shifts ontologically as it unfolds, it never abandons some sort of reportorial claim.

Most important, however, and the reason "A zokn" occupies a central position in the early canon, is its near-seemless yoking of conventions of the most disparate nature. One almost forgets how rapidly the narrative locus passes from Krochmalna Street in Warsaw during a specific, identifiable, and recent period of months well-remembered by a majority of contemporary readers (i.e. from an historical setting with extratextual constraints) to a never-never land in which hundred-year-old men father children with middle-aged widows. A bit paradoxically, perhaps, even the fairy-tale quality of the story's conclusion – and the literary burdening of the text as a whole – serve a defictionalizing function vis-à-vis the protagonist: the unreality of Janow regained invites the reader to forget that Moyshe-Ber is himself a character in a distinctly fictional short story with a highly improbable plot. That is to say, Singer emphasizes the fictiveness of the allusive vehicle in order to posit the nonfictiveness of the embedded tenor. Not that he need succeed in this attempt: the point is not to convince the reader to naturalize the text as the chronicle its subtitle asserts it to be but, rather, to convince the reader that there is nothing particularly problematic about a text which moves without comment among worlds the basic givens of which so radically differ from one another.

Singer accomplished much in "A zokn"; it was not, however, without a price: the mixing of fictive and non-fictive elements was only achieved at the expense of an insistent bookishness which, by burdening the text with references not to life but to life as filtered by other literary texts, actually undermines what is otherwise its primary thesis. For the assertion that fantastic and mundane elements may coexist in purely literary texts is undoubtedly true, but irrelevant; Singer would argue, rather, that they coexist unmediated and this, in turn, appears to call for texts of less overt bookishness. It is possible that Singer simply was not yet sufficiently accomplished to attempt texts at once contemporary in setting and more than marginally fictitious in mode. For most of the succeeding decades, Singer was to concentrate on writing reportage as fiction, though not before publishing an extremely interesting historical novel, *Der zindiker meshiekh* [The

Sinning Messiah], with which his early oeuvre, and my discussion thereof, concludes.

IV

Taken as a whole, Singer's early fictions reveal a clear predisposition toward contemporary settings. "Eyniklekh" and "Sale," as well as all but two other works in the Polish canon, take place in geographically – and, for the most part, chronologically – precise settings in contemporary Poland.[31] Only when he turned his attention from general experiments with rewriting works in received genres to the more specific task of integrating fantastic and quotidien elements did Singer feel compelled to remove his texts from contemporary, real-world frames of reference. We have seen how this was accomplished in "A zokn." But even where the text (and reader) is not brought all the way back to biblical times, settings were displaced to an indeterminate – frequently rural and hasidic – location before the fantastic was allowed entry into the fiction. In "Oyfn oylem-hatoye" [In the World of Chaos], for example, a young man feels increasingly ill at ease in urban Warsaw. On an extended and not always lucidly-recounted journey from rural hasidic court to rural hasidic court (the narrative is largely in narrated monologue [erlebte Rede], the character upon whom it is focused incoherent and perhaps already dead),[32] the fantastic intrudes in inverse proportion to the amount of real-worldly orientation given in the narrative. By the time the young man is told to look under his shirt, see that he's already dressed in winding sheets, and find a grave to lie down in, we are at a hasidic court which might as well have been in the seventeenth as in the twentieth century.[33]

Singer's single lengthy foray into fantasy was Der sotn in Goray: A mayse fun fartsaytns [Satan in Goray: A Tale of Bygone Days], a short novel important in ways not immediately relevant to this investigation.[34] More interesting than its contents, at least for my purpose, is its setting (fartsaytns [bygone days]) and its generic tag (mayse [tale], rather than roman [novel] or novele [novella]). Singer is, apparently, willing to admit of the possibility of supernatural intervention in human affairs, but only when that intervention is held at both generic and chronological remove. This is, in fact, strikingly reminiscent of Nathaniel Hawthorne's dilemma in *The House of the Seven Gables* and *The Blithedale Romance*,[35] for Hawthorne, too, saw the fantastic and the quotidien as inversely related.

We remember that *The House of the Seven Gables* was set in a location fully as isolated, if not quite as historically remote, as Singer's Goray. In his preface to the novel, Hawthorne claims generic dispensation by emphasizing that his work was not a novel but a romance — as Singer's was not a *roman* but a *mayse*:

> When a writer calls his work a Romance, it need hardly be observed that he wished to claim a certain latitude, both as to its fashion and material, which he would not have felt himself entitled to assume had he professed to be writing a Novel. The latter form of composition is presumed to aim at a very minute fidelity, not merely to the possible, but to the probable and ordinary course of man's experience. The former — while as a work of art, it must rigidly subject itself to laws, and while it sins unpardonably so far as it may swerve aside from the truth of the human heart — has fairly a right to present that truth under circumstances, to a great extent, of the writer's own choosing or creation. . . . He will be wise, no doubt, to make a very moderate use of the prividleges here stated, and, especially, to mingle the Marvelous rather as a slight, delicate, and evanescent flavor, than as any portion of the actual substance of the dish offered to the public. He can hardly be said, however, to commit a literary crime even if he disregard this caution.[36] (January 1851)

Only sixteen months later, Hawthorne was to take a major — and, for him, daring — step by setting a longer fiction in a nearly undisguised analogue of Brook Farm (lest the reader otherwise overlook the allusion, Hawthorne makes it explicit in the preface), which flourished "now a little more than ten years ago." As an author, Hawthorne explains, he sought a location "a little removed from the highway of ordinary travel, where the creatures of his brain may play their phantasmagorial antics, without exposing them to too close a comparison with the actual events of real lives."[37] Hawthorne was never quite to reconcile the demands of fantasy and contemporaneousness; as late as December 1859, he was still lamenting the difficulty of doing so in his preface to *The Marble Faun*.[38]

Singer had, for his part, already produced works set in contemporary Poland, on the one hand, or either set or receding toward a decidedly non-contemporary past, Polish or otherwise, on the other. Both approaches had generated important texts which made new use of inherited genres while undermining generic norms. Singer had yet to tackle the one long fictional form which made simultaneous claim to fictiveness and literal historicity – the historical novel.[39] This was a tremendously popular form with origins at least as far back in Yiddish literary history as the early nineteenth century. Indeed, Sholom Aleichem's complaint about the alleged non-Jewishness of Yiddish fiction in the latter decades of that century were based more on the currency of the historical novel – whether in serialization, as was customary in the heyday of Ayzik-Meyer Dik, or in tripledecker format, as popularized by Shaykevitsh – than on works with contemporary but foreign settings.[40] A culling of my rather random collection of pre-World War I popular novels turns up two such titles: *Der baron un di markize: A hekhst-interesanter roman* [The Baron and the Marchioness: A Highly Interesting Novel] by Shaykevitsh[41] and *Malke veHadase: Eyn zeyer fayner historisher roman, eyne vare geshikhte fun eyne yidishe meydkhen vos var di tokhter fun dem Mister Yossen vos var groys-shatsmayster bay Haynrikh dem tsveytn kinig fun England in di tsaytn fun gzeyres oykh iz do fun onfang eyne herlekhe hagdome, vos balebt dize ertseylung vi dem kerper di neshome* [Malke and Hadassah: A Very fine Historical Novel, a True Story of a Jewish Girl Who Was the Daughter of Mister Yossen, Who Was Chancellor of the Exchequer to Henry II, King of England in the time of the Evil Decree of 1096; At the Beginning Is Also a Wonderful Introduction Which Gives Life to This Story as the Soul Does the Body] by A.-M. D. (= Ayzik-Meyer Dik or one of his imitators?).[42] This is not to say that more overtly Jewish themes did not predominate. *Pace* Sholom Aleichem, historical novels such as Shaykevitsh's *Di geheyme yidn: A roman fun der yidisher geshikhte in Shpanyen* [The Secret Jews: A Novel About Jewish History in Spain][43] were more the norm. Though a definitive history of the Yiddish historical novel is long overdue,[44] there is no doubt that its popularity continued unabated into the 1930s, when it was a staple of both the European and American Yiddish press. To this day, Yude Elberg's historical potboilers remain a predictable feature of the *Forverts*.

In this context, one might expect Singer's own historical novel to have begun publication unheralded, especially considering the author's still modest reputation in the United Sates: Singer had published only two short pieces in New York by 5 October 1935, when serialization of *Der zindiker meshiekh: Historisher roman* [The Sinning Messiah: An Historical Novel] commenced.[45] Neither the author nor his announced genre would, then, have attracted particular attention, especially in light of the novel's midweek publication schedule (as a rule, Tuesdays and Thursdays, though even this relatively low-priority allocation of space was subject to occasional preemption). Thus it must have been startling when Ab. Kan (Abraham Cahan), editor of the *Forverts*, announced the appearance of *Der zindiker meshiekh* with atypical fanfare. Under his own byline, he wrote an introductory article of impressive format: four half-columns above the fold with a serpentine banner headline: "Yankev Frank: Der firer fun der yidisher sekte, velkhe hot gepredikt, az mit zind un oysgelasnkayt vet men aropbrengen meshiekhn (Onshtot a hagdome tsum realistish-historishn roman *Der zindiker meshiekh)*" [Yankev Frank, the Leader of the Jewish Sect that Taught that Sin and Depravity Would Bring the Messiah (In Lieu of an Introduction to the Realistic Historical Novel, *The Sinning Messiah)*].

The introduction (in characteristically Germanized Yiddish) asserts that

dos iz a spetsyeler sort roman un a derklerung vegn zayn kharakter vet do zayn nit iberik . . . Di, vos zaynen gut bakant mit der yidishe[r] geshikhte . . . zaynen gut bakant mit der zonderbarer, kimat ibernatirlekher, tetikayt vos er [Yankev Frank] hot ongefirt. . . . File bikher un on a tsol artiklen oyf farsheydene shprakhen zaynen vegn dem tsezeyt un tseshpreyt. Der yidisher shriftshteler Yitskhok Bashevis hot dizn materyal durkhgeshtudiert. . . . Derbay muz men bamerkn, as Bashevis iz a shriftshteler fun dem sort, velkhe hobn a rikhtikn khush. Er hot di feikayt optsuteyln virklekhkayt fun puste[r] fantazye. Dem "Zindikn meshiekh"

shraybt Bashevis oyfn grunt fun al di dermonte materyaln un mit
der hilf fun dem dermontn khush farn emes. Es iz a roman, er
iz ober durkhoys oyfgeboyt oyf faktn.
[this is a special kind of novel and a statement about its character
would not be out of place. . . . Those who are well acquainted with
Jewish history . . . know well the extraordinary, almost supernatural activities which he (Yankev Frank) directed. Many books
and countless articles in various languages are scattered far and
wide. The Yiddish Writer Yitskhok Bashevis has studied these
materials thoroughly. . . . In this regard one must notet that
Bashevis is one of those writers who have a genuine sense (khush).
He has the ability to separate truth from empty fantasy. Bashevis
has written *The Sinning Messiah* on the basis of the above materials
and with the help of the above-mentioned sense of truth. It is a
novel, but one completely based on facts.][46]

Singer has, both by his choice of subject matter and, more
explicitly, by use of a generic tag as subtitle, encouraged the reader
to naturalize his text as conventional historical novel. Nonetheless,
Kan insists upon modifying the generic tag from *historisher roman*
[historical novel] to *realistish-historisher roman* [realistic historical
novel], emphasizing thereby the work's claim to literal historicity; this is also the thrust of his introductory note. We should,
moreover, not that *Der zindiker meshiekh*, alone of the historical
novels published in the *Forverts* during the three decades for
which there is reliable data, appears on the op-ed pages, and not
on the *romanzayt* [novel page] or in the Sunday literary supple-
ment. Kan was not – could not have been – reacting solely to the
claims of historical fidelity, since that is a generic constant (the
claim, not the fidelity!); nor, on the other hand, could he have
been adverse to fictiveness (*fantazye*) per se: the *Forverts* published
short stories, novellas, and *humoreskn* [humorous sketches] in its
literary pages which lay no claim to historical veracity or even
verisimilitude. It was, rather, the unmediated juxtaposition of
historical and novelistic elements which, I believe, occasioned
Kan's apparent malaise while at the same time exciting his interest.[47] Though Kan, for commercial reasons if none other, chose
to voice his reservations in the most glowing of terms, he had,
independently it would seem, rederived the English historical
novel's earlier "crisis of confidence" discussed by Amanda Alonso:

Its utility as history, as historically accurate information, tends to contravene its ability to delight as fiction, and vice versa. Its strengths as history deny it the virtues of imaginative writing. Is it then merely a hybrid offspring of history and the novel, and therefore without the generative lasting force of the purer strains?[48]

The early chapters of *Der zindiker meshiekh* do little to still a reader's malaise with the hybrid nature of the historical novel as genre, with what Murray Baumgarten identifies as "the tension between historical description/evocation and fictive character, event, and scene-making."[49] To the contrary—they reflect Singer's by now familiar strategy of recapitulating generic norms while invoking these norms in their starkest form. If the general strategy is familiar, *Der zindiker meshiekh* demonstrates a remakably innovative approach to balancing fictive and historical elements within a single work—their assignment to different chapters with alternating, though unnamed and only partially characterized, narrators.

Although I would like to presuppose familiarity on my readers' part with this novel, or at least a willingness to examine the original text, to do so would be to honor the conventions of scholarship while ignoring their underlying rationale: Singer has nowhere alluded to *Der zindiker meshiekh*; his anglophone critics are, as I discuss in the final chapter, wholly dependent upon interviews with him for information about untranslated works; the Yiddish scholarly community has lacked both collected editions and bio-bibliographical tools. Hence the existence of this novel has been one of its author's secrets.[50] Inevitably, then, I shall have to preface a consideration of narrative strategy in *Der zindiker meshiekh* with rather more plot-summary than would otherwise be necessary or advisable.

Chapter One begins in the Ashkenazic synagogue in Bucharest; the date is not stated but, from internal evidence, is somewhere in the early eighteenth century—perhaps around 1740. Although an ordinary weekday, both the (men's) central synagogue area and the women's balcony have full attendance at afternoon prayers; candles are burning in the hanging lamps and candelabras, as on the High Holidays. The congregants wear prayer shawls over their heads and are universally pale and drawn, whether from the unusual fast which has been called by the rabbinate or from the news which has occasioned it: persecutions throughout the Jewish world are on a cruel increase – forced exile and burning of holy books in Hungary, blood libels in Bohemia, pious Jews buried alive in Poland, murder of penitants at the Western Wall in Jerusalem. Situated at the crossroads of trade and immigration routes, Bucharest collects both the news and the refugees of these dislocations.

An unusually tall man – at least a head taller than the average congregant – bony, with a swarthy complexion like Yemenite's, a long pointed beard, fiery eyes, a sable cap and long silk robes, appears at the synagogue door. He does not wait for an attendant to show him a fitting place, but immediately takes a seat of honor at the eastern wall, beginning a series of strange prayers full of odd body movements, bows, and near-prostrations. Though his personal magnetism attracts the congregants' gaze, the stranger ignores his surroundings, barely acknowledging the presence of the old rabbi, Reb Ayzikl, who, unable to retain control of the services, approaches the stranger with a number of questions. To these, the stranger replies with laconic indifference. Reb Ayzikl, suddenly enraged, pulls the prayer shawl from the stranger's head, bids his sexton bring a staff and thongs to bind the stranger, and begins to tremble uncontrollably. The prominent congregants intervene, astounded at their rabbie's behavior. Only when Reb Ayzikl explains that the stranger is an unrependent follower of the layte Shapsi Tsvi (Sabbatai Zevi) does the congregation rally to his commands; many decades earlier, before the false messiah had been exposed, Reb Ayzikl had led the stranger to the city gates and into exile.

The stranger protests his innocence in an oddly detached, mildly amused manner, daring the congregants to lay hands upon him. When it appears that they would indeed do so, a young, local ne'er-do-well named Yankev (Frank?) springs to the stranger's aid, threatening to split open the head of anyone who stands in the way of their retreat. Stunned, the congregants let the two pass and exit.

Der zindiker meshiekh is told by a third-person, anonymous narrator. Yet the narrator's omniscience is curiously circumscribed and, in several respects, he functions more as character than as convention. This, in turn, has direct bearing on the degree to which Singer is willing to appropriate historical materials and fashion fictions out of them.

In general, the narrator enjoys a perspective somewhat broader than do the novel's other characters. He begins at some remove from his material: while the congregants are anxiously and animatedly praying, he calmly surveys the synagogue's appearance and that of th econgregation, reporting his observations to the reader. On the other hand, he is privy to no data to which another congregant would not have access. Thus the reader is not informed, and cannot be, of the stranger's identity. This does not seem merely to be a device to increase suspense employed by the narrator (though it is surely that on Singer's part) but, more importantly, a consistent limitation of perspective to that of an eighteenth-century Jew from Bucharest. The nonvolitional quality of the narrator's circumscription is emphasized by the straightforward chronological unfolding of the action. Time sequences are not violated, though they are held in occasional abeyance while the reader receives necessary background information – why there is such activity at midweek, for example. Nor is there any warning about sudden actions such as Reb Ayzikl's changed demeanor or Frank's violent interruption.

This narrative situation is by no means uncommon; indeed, it is repeated in dozens of stories and is a familiar device for drawing the reader into the world of the book. Here, however, it also serves to undermine the fictiveness of the reported action, as I shall attempt to demonstrate. On the one hand, the plot is clearly a fictive one: Reb Ayzikl, the stranger, and young Frank have no extratextual existence nor, even if the reader had privileged access to data on eighteenth-century Bucharest, could he or she confirm th veracity of the reported events. On the other hand, Bucharest and Yankev Frank surely have extratextual correlates and, especially in light of Kan's introductory comments, the readership is well within its prerogatives in measuring the events by the yardstick of historical documentation. Furthermore, the historicity of the narrator and fictional narrative are asserted by the limited omniscience the narrator is permitted. And though he is unnamed and not, it would seem, physically present in the synagogue, his actions emphasize his character-like quality.

Describing the synagogue at the chapter's beginning, for example, he writes: "In shul hot geshmekt met kheylev un mit vaks, vi yonkiper farnakht tsu nile. . . ." [The synagogue smelled of tallow and wax, like Yom Kippur evening at the Nehila service.] Narrative conventions do not have a sense of smell, nor are they apt to seek similes from their own experiences. Here the narrator resembles a contemporary chronicler or memoirist – an eyewitness, as it were, to the story's veracity.

Notwithstanding his character-like qualities, the narrator assumes absolute authority for the phenomena he observes personally, and glosses their import with eighteenth-century cosmology:

> Oyser dem hobn zikh in himl bavizn tseykhns, vos hobn keyn guts nisht ongezogt. Bay nakht hot men gezen a shtern mit a langen ek, vos hot oysgezen vi a fayerdike rut. Dos iz geven a simen, as got tsornt oyf der velt un az er vet zi shtrofn. Alte vayber hobn dertseylt, az zey hobn gezen in himl bay zun-untergang a fayerdikn rayter oyf a fayerdik ferd. In der hant hot er gehaltn a shpiz. dos iz geven a tseykhn oyf milkhomes un blut-fargisung. [Besides, signs appeared in the sky which foretold no good. People saw a star at night with a long tail which looked like a fiery rod. This was a sign that God was angry with the world and wanted to punish it. Old wives told how they saw in the sunset a fiery rider on a fiery horse. In his hand he held a spear. It was a portent of wars and bloodbaths to come.]

The narrator's position on the veracity of the reports, as well as on their portent, is difficult to pin down. The first sentence quoted above is in his own voice: he vouches both for the appearance of the signs and for their predictive value. But, although he is willing to go on record that signs of some sort had appeared, he does not offer himself as eyewitness; not he, but *men* [one, they, people] saw the star – the gloss of its meaning is, in all probability, narrated monologue, though the narrator does not expressly distance himself from the sighting. On the other hand, only *alte vayber* [old wives] reported seeing the fiery rider and horse. But why, if this is so, does he dwell upon the meaning of an event the existence of which he tacityly doubts? Is this another example of narrated monologue or is it, as I suspect, a further instance of hedged fictionality, with the narrator protecting his credibility as historian (and, ipso facto, Singer's as well) among skeptical readers while letting believers feel he shares their apprehension?

To summarize, then, the first installment of *Der zindiker meshiekh* exhibits elements of diverse, and nearly contradictory, direction – although the juxtaposition of these elements is neither unique nor even especially unusual (one thinks of texts as diverse as the *Nibelungenlied* and *Catch-22*). On the one hand, historicity is emphasized by the narrative perspecitve and by the provision of concrete geographical and chronological referents. On the other hand, fictiveness is emphasized by the high degree of artifice in the work. The structure permits the reader such double perspective, rather than tying him or her to the perspecitve of the action or to that of the narrator who reports it. And, finally, the context reinforced both tendencies: though *Der zindiker meshiekh* appears, as we have noted, on the news and political commentary pages of the *Forverts*, its structure is that of installment fiction – a daily reminder of the novel's status as novel. Here artifice functions both to organize reality and to draw attention to the essential literariness of organized reality.

Here Singer both honors and exploits the conventions of the historical novel.[51] What is unusual in *Der zindiker meshiekh* is Singer's choice to point up, rather than suppress or simply ignore, the problematicness of the historical novel as genre. To be sure, hedged claims to historicity are, willy-nilly, concomitants of those historical fictions which deal with society in synchronic cross-section. Speaking of Scott's Waverly novels, for example, Alexander Welsh concludes that "the inclusive picture of society . . . does not result from a collection of data from all walks of life, but from the contrast of styles."[52] But Singer does not merely write in contrasting styles; he assigns, as I shall show, successive chapters to entirely different narrators with radically different perspectives.

The second installment, after a rather long summary of the one which preceded it, begins as follows:

Ver es iz geven Shapsi Tsvi hot men tsu yener tsayt gut gevust in Bukaresht, un nisht bloyz in Bukaresht aleyn, in ale lender vu yidn hobn nor ongeshpart, hot men nokh alts gedenkt ver es iz Shapsi Tsvi un vos er hot geton.
[They all knew well who Shapsi Tsvi was in Bucharest, and not

in Bucharest alone; in every country where Jews had settled, they
still remembered who Shapsi Tsvi was and what he did.][53]

At no point does this chapter proper refer to the previous one;
not even the characters or situation is mentioned. Though this
is not unusual in popular historical fiction, the summary which
occupies the installment's first two columns would certainly lead
the reader to expect a degree of continuity – at least in narrative
perspective, if not in the matter of reported incident. But, in fact,
there is a radical shift in both the narrator's perspective and omniscience. The perspective is much broader than that of the first
chapter – activities of the Tsviites over the entire expanse of Jewish
Europe and the Orient are reported with no trailing off of accuracy or detail with distance from Bucharest. We remember that
the narrator of the first installment, though unnamed and not
quite a participant in the action, was very close to that action,
even to the point of recording sensory impressions of the events.
This narrator remains detached from the actions he records: the
effects of the Tsviite movement are not described in personal
terms (that is, in terms of their consequences for specific individuals) but, rather, in terms of the consequences for undifferen-
tiated groups of adherents and detractors. And, whereas the narrator of the first installment referred to unnamed individuals, with
two exceptions, as *yidn* [Jews, people], emphasizing both their
human aspect and his sense of community with them, the narrator of the second installment refers to unnamed individuals as
men [they, people, one], thereby emphasizing actions (verbs),
rather than initiators or recipients of actions (nouns), and, even
more importantly, excluding himself from the communities of
which he speaks.

By assigning this chapter to an uncharacterized narrative
voice who speaks with unimpeachable authority on historical
matters, Singer again pushes his historical fiction toward historical
reportage. The neutral authority of th enarrator is underscored
by contrast with the cautiously engaged, though far less privileged, narrator of the first chapter. Once again, however, the effect
is mixed: if this narrator speaks with greater authority within the
fictional frame, the reader is reminded by the abrupt change of
narrator that *Der zindiker meshiekh* is, at base, a fiction in which
the author is free to manipulate character, narrator, and historical

fact to suit artistic (i.e. fictional), rather than historiographic, purpose.

Here, again, Singer stands within the tradition but at its very borders. On the one hand, shifting narrative focus is a touchstone of the historical novel. As Murray Baumgarten writes:

> If history is now conceived of as a culture of a particular time and place as it manifests itself in the texture and life of an entire people, then the writer tests the ideals of institutions and cultures by the realities of historical events and crises through the medium of imagined, representative characters in typical conflict.[54]

On the other hand, the "imagined, representative characters" of Singer's choosing are not, save to the critically sophisticated, characters at all, but rather anonymous narrative voices. In short, rather than viewing a large and shifting cast of characters through consistent narrative eyes, we view a more circumscribed set of characters through shifting narrative eyes. The approach is even more extreme in the third installment, which reurns to the previously-introduced characters in Bucharest.

Though less focused and ultimately less interesting than the earlier two chapters in its juxtaposition of fictiveness and historicity, the third chapter warrants mention if only because it contains yet another shift in narrative voice. Here the narrator is omniscient, but more inclined to exercise that omniscience in matters personal and proximate, rather than historical. He reveals first information known only to Reb Ayzikl (the cause of Reb Ayzikl's enmity toward the stranger, who had occasioned his young wife's death), then information unknown to any of those present in the Bucharest synagogue (the stranger's name, Yosef ben Khosid). But he is also the most characterized of the narrators, even though we do not learn much about him. He is, first, an engaged anti-Tsviite, assuming that the reader will know who is meant by the epithet *klovim* [curs]: "Reb Ayzikl hot oykh gevust," he tels us, "az in Bukaresht gefinden zikh biz tsum hayntikn tog klovim." [Reb Ayzikl also knew that curs have remained in Bucharest even to the present day.][55] Second, as is evident from the cited passage, he is an actual resident of eighteenth-century Bucharest (unlike the initial narrator, who limited himself to reporting observed action in the synagogue but whose status as community member was belied by a reportorial neutrality): he even writes in the present tense – unusual and not a little odd-sounding in Yiddish narrative – further underscoring his contemporaneousness with the events he narrates. Considered logically within the context of the fiction, this third narrator is most perplexing in his prerogatives: he is utterly omniscient but has the values and personality of a historical character. Although this fundamental inconsistency cannot be subsumed in a reading which makes sense of the narrative situation, it is, I suspect, an allusion to – and reconstruction of – the typical narrative mode of *Forverts* historical romance. By the end of the third chapter, then, Singer has come full circle, having broken away from the *hekhst-interesante* historical novelistic tradition only to embrace it at last, justifying the work's generic tag at the expense of his editor's attempt to make of it a work of a different kind.

Indeed, the novel continues to move – not always seamlessly – between the poles documented historiography and popular historical fiction. If, by its latter third, much of the historiographical baggage has been jettisoned in favor of a more overt approach, *Der zindiker meshiekh* remains within limits imposed both by the author's project and by his readers' independent knowledge of at least the major facets of Frank's career. Moreover, the three narrative consciousnesses (and, with trifling exceptions, only these three) alternate with one another through the novel's conclusion some forty installments later.

Somewhat curiously, perhaps, the shifting narrative modes themselves lend historical veracity to the narrative material and help counter the drift toward fictiveness: portraying three distinct consciousnesses attempting to come to terms with the same data (and reporting yet other attempts to make sense of an unusually complex set of events) works to validate the extraliterary veracity of the data itself – else why would it merit such detailed and persistent investigation and reinvestigation? Singer thus effects a radical and rather remarkable transformation: by emphasizing the artifice and conventionality of narration, the artifice and conventionality of fiction itself is abscured. Multiple narrators cannot, we are told, alter the "truth" of the events they cronicle.

With *Der zindiker meshiekh* two parallel developments in Singer's creative career come to fruition. First, Singer has proven his mastery of an impressive variety of inherited genres – minimalist fiction, *reportazh*, travel chronicle, historical novel – and has settled accounts with at least some of the important Yiddish writers whose works, and reputations, preceded his own. Indeed, generic tags disappear almost entirely from Singer's works for nearly a decade, and the question of genre is not raised explicitly until publication of the "Author's Note" prefacing the English edition of *Mayn tatns bezdn-shtub* (*In My Father's Court*);[56] though later works allude unmistakably to works by other major writers – one thinks immediately of Singer counterpieces to Lamed Shapiro's "Der rov un di rebetsn" [The Rabbi and the Rabbi's Wife][57] or to Sholom Aleichem's stories narrated by barnyard fowl[58] – Singer's early, nearly obsessive concern with inherited genres was to wane as his own art matured. During the next decade, Singer was to concentrate on another general strategy, the inverse of his approach during the first decade of his career – writing reportage as fiction. And it is to this strategy which we now turn.

Chapter 2

Reportage as Fiction, I:
Singer's Pseudonymous Personas

Singer had, by 1936, reached a dead end of sorts. Although he continued to publish short pieces in the *Forverts* through mid-1937, they were, in terms of narrative strategy, no more interesting or sophisticated than the work he was doing immediately before and following his emigration to America – nor were they, qualitatively, distinguished. It is not surprising that this should be so: with "A zokn" Singer had analyzed a short story into its allusive constituents, and with *Der zindiker meshiekh* he had exploited the conventions of the historical novel so as to put into question the work's authority both as history and as novel. The element common to the Singer's literary oeuvre from his initial appearance in the *Literarishe bleter* through the second hiatus in his productive career in 1937[1] was, as I have argued in the previous chapter, the attempt to shade fiction into reportage. This strategy had to be laid aside for a time – for nearly a decade, as it turned out – not because Singer's literary abilities were not equal to continuing this experiment, for after the radical experimentation of "A zokn" and *Der zindiker meshiekh*, only works of unabashedly avant-garde cast remained as immediate possibilities. And this, in turn, was a priori unacceptable: Singer might write experimental fiction but, as an outspoken opponent of the avant-garde[2] his fictions had at least to look like conventional works in recognizable genres.

In Chapter Four, I discuss the discrepancies between Singer's interview statements and the actual facts of his creative career – as well as the reasons for and uses of these discrepancies; here I should like only to point out that there is usually a germ of truth behind most, if not quite all, of Singer's invented and inventive autobiography. Though there was no years-long period of literary unproductivity, as he has often asserted,[3] and none at all when he claims there to have been, there was a two-year hiatus in his productive career – from mid-1937 through mid-1939.[4] When Singer was to resume writing, it would be under a new pseudonym and with a substantially new narrative strategy – the inverse, in fact, of the one he had employed for the previous twelve years.

Before turning to this new period, however, it might be useful to consider the functions of the pseudonym under which Singer had published all but his very first work of fiction – Yitskhok Bashevis. The genesis of the pseudonym was prosaic enough: Singer wished to avoid confusion on the part of his readers between himself and his older brother, also Y. Zinger. This was not without precedent in Yiddish literary circles: one thinks, for example, of Leyvik Halper, who adopted the pseudonym H. Leyvik to preclude confusion with his better-established elder, Moyshe-Leyb Halpern. In Singer's case, as in Leyvik's, there was no notion of persona-building by adopting a pseudonym: though critics have speculated – none too productively, I fear – on the reasons Singer rejected his (father's) surname in favor of a word-play clearly alluding to his mother (*Bashevis* is nearly homophonous with *Bas-sheves*; his mother's name was Bathsheba – or, in Yiddish, *Bas-sheve*, and the final *s* a possessive marker, as in English), Yitskhok Bashevis is only in the most technical sense a pseudonym; no one was in doubt that the historical Yitskhok Zinger produced the texts attributed to Yitskhok Bashevis. There was no distance, no ironic interplay between the Bashevis who was, by virtue of his works' signature or byline their putative author and the Zinger who was universally known to be their author.[5] Indeed, the Yitskhok Bashevis of these early pieces might better be regarded as signature than as pseudonym – surely not as persona. As such, the matter would not have been worth the pages to tell of it were that signature not to gain new vitality and function in light of Singer's immeasurably more interesting creation of a true persona—the initial appearance of Yitskhok Varshavski in 1939.

I

Singer has made no secret that many of his works were originally ascribed to Yitskhok Varshavski; he speaks at some length about the pseudonym in a number of interviews, and even mentions it in the Author's Note prefacing *In My Father's Court*.[6] Indeed, this is one of the few facts of his Yiddish publishing career which Singer has chosen to share with his English-language readership. Singer would have his readers believe that the difference between Bashevis and Varshavski is essentially a matter of the care with which he prepares and edits a particular manuscript. His earliest articulation of this view came in a 1963 interview with Joel Blocker and Richard Elman:

> Occasionally, however, I write more popular work under a different name—Warshofsky. Generally I sign my name in the *Forward* Isaac Bashevis, but once in a while I publish under the name Isaac Warshofsky. When I write under the name Warshofsky I take less care, but I never publish such things in book form. . . . It sometimes happens that some of them come out well. In fact, one of my books is . . . a compilation of this kind of work, published under the name Warshofsky. Only later I adopted it, as it were, and signed the name Bashevis . . . after I cleaned it up and worked on it . . .[7]

A year later, Singer reiterated and elaborated on this view in a "conversation" with Marshall Breger and Bob Barnhart in which the interviewers allude to the earlier interview:

> *I also understand that you write for a deadline under a slightly different name—Warshavsky. I wonder if you could tell me something about this . . .*
>
> Warshavsky is actually my journalistic pen name. When I write under *Warshavsky* I don't worry too much about style. I just write because I have to write, because I am connected with a newspaper.[8]

Singer is a good deal more cautious in his reply to Chone Shmeruk's written query of 1973:

> Di grenets tsvishn Bashevis un Varshavski iz mit der tsayt gevorn farvisht. In onheyb hot Varshavski gezolt shraybn "laykhtere zahkn", ober vi bald beyde zenen nemen fun zelben mentsh, iz der stil ariber fun eynem tsum andern. . . . Di kvalitet iz oft geven di zelbe. Ikh volt gezogt as Varshavski hot a bisl veyniker akhtung geton oyf der shprakh. . . . Ober oft hob ikh punkt azoy geshilfn a Varshavski-dertseylung. [The border between Bashevis and Varshavski has become less clear with time. At the outset Varshavski was to have written "lighter pieces," but since both names belong to the same person, the style of one merged with that of the other. . . . The quality was often the same. I'd say that Varshavski paid a bit less attention to his use of language. . . . . But often I polished a Varshavski story every bit as much (as one by Bashevis).][9]

At first glance, Singer appears to be deferring to – and protecting himself – from Shmeruk's detailed knowledge of his oeuvre: unlike the pairs of anglophone interviewers, Singer's sometime Yiddish editor and chair of Israel's most distinguished Yiddish department could not fail to question Singer's distinction between the Bashevis and Varshavski signatures, at least in the uncompromising terms of the English interviews. But what would appear to be a frank and measured (re)consideration, even a retreat of sorts from his earlier assertions, is only a more subtle attempt at dissimulation. For, though he is more sympathetic toward Varshavski's efforts in his letter to Shmeruk, Singer continues to maintain that Bashevis writes for deadline-free publication and Varshavski for the press, that Bashevis accordingly enjoys the privilege of leisurely revision frequently denied Varshavski – and that therein lies the difference between them.

Neither Singer's characterization of Varshavski nor the contrast he draws between him and Bashevis can withstand measure against the oeuvre. To begin with the latter, we remember that the sixty-five pieces Singer wrote between 1925 and 1937 were all signed Bashevis, regardless of their genre (short story, minimalist fiction, reportage, critical article, book review, occasional piece) or forum (literary weekly, anthology, daily newspaper, book). By contrast, Bashevis all but disappears in 1939, ceding he space in the *Forverts* to Varshavski; his was not to return to its pages until 1945, with a serialization of *Di familye Mushkat* (*The Family Moskat*).[10] It is, in short, difficult to consider Bashevis and Varshavski in contrastive terms—at least with regard to the care with which they edited their pieces—since each pseudonym was developed in the absence of the other.

Why, then, did Singer feel it necessary to abandon one name and adopt another? Or, to rephrase the question somewhat, how did Varshavski differ from Bashevis? The difference, as I hope to demonstrate, was both ontological and functional: Varshavski had a different mode of existence than had Bashevis, and he wrote about different matters to different ends.

Unlike Bashevis, which was, transparently, the literary signature of the real-world Isaac Singer and did not—could not by nature—stand in anything but one-to-one juxtaposition with its inventor, Varshavski was a persona without extra-literary referent. Indeed, Singer made a single but very suggestive attempt to supply an extratectual existence for Varshavski distinct from that of Bashevis-Singer. In "A yidisher shrayber makht an onklage kegn a yidishn farlag" [A Yiddish Writer Registers a Complaint Against a Yiddish Publisher],[11] Varshavski complains on Bashevis' behalf that the Farlag Matones has withheld royalty payments on *Der sotn in Goray* (*Satan in Goray*) in order to, the publisher claims, support others of its titles. The pseudonymous play is rather cautious: Varshavski doesn't state how he learned of the publisher's highhandedness—one misses a description of Bashevis through Varshavski's eyes—nor, in fact, do the third-person reference to the "Yiddish writer" expressly preclude the knowledgeable if literally-minded reader from identifying Varshavski with Bashevis-Singer. (By September 1946, when the letter appears, Varshavski had been writing for nearly eight years and his identity must have been an open secret in Yiddish cultural circles, at least.) On the other hand, the headline writer (possibly Ab. Kan [Cahan], considering the article's content), abets the persona-building by appending the subtitle gloss: "A briv fun undzer mitarbeter Yitskhok Varshavski" [A Letter from Our Colleague Yitskhok Varshavski]; the *Forverts*, as institution and in its unmistakably ponderous collective voice, here claims personhood for

Varshavski – a not insubstantial boost to Singer's own, more cautious efforts in the same direction.

Though Singer wrote Shmeruk that "in onheyb hot Varshavski gezolt shraybn 'laykhtere zakhn'" [at the outset Varshavski was to have written "lighter pieces"], Varshavski's early oeuvre included such decidedly earnest pieces as "An interesante debate: Hot Hitler vild gemakht Daytshland oder der 'daytsher gayst' hot geshafn Hitlern?" [An Interesting Controversy: Did Hitler Uncivilize Germany or Did the German Spirit Create Hitler?], "Der heldisher kamf fun yidn kegn di natsis in der varshever geto" [Heroic Battle of Jews Against Nazis in the Warsaw Ghetto], "Di yidishe shprakh un kultur lebt iber ir greste krizis" [Yiddish Language and Culture Undergo Their Greatest Crisis], "Stsenes fun yomerlekhn dales in Varshe" [Scenes of Bitter Poverty in Warsaw], "Hitlers geshray az er firt milkhomes kegn yidn" [Hitler's Battle Cry Against the Jews].[12] While the more strictly reportorial of these articles are not entirely typical of Varshavski's porduction – it took a bit of rummaging among the bibliographical entries to turn them up – both the seriousness in tone and content and the early dates of their publication belie Singer's characterization of the function initially assigned Varshavski.

Only once in his later interviews did Singer let slip an important aspect of his Varshavski signature – that it represents, indeed is the primary agent of, his process of persona-building:

> *Did you find a conscious shift in your methods or techniques when you decide to write under one name or the other?*
> (. . .) A pen name is very important for a writer. It is a different kind of ego. It is a kind of second personality.[13]

Though I should not want to make too much of Singer's exact phrasing here, it is interesting to note that he speaks of Varshavski as a second, and not a third, personality. for, as I have argued, Bashevis and Varshavski are ontologically quite dissimilar: the former inheres in an historical author who creates texts, the latter wholly within texts which, in turn, create their putative author. Drawing this distinction is not mere exercise; Varshavski, at least, has only his texts with which to pursue his narrative strategies. Before examining a specific text rather closely, however, it would be useful to survey the hundred-odd pieces signed Varshavski between Bashevis' eclipse in 1937 and the emergence of yet another pseudonymous persona in 1943. How, specifically, does Singer go about building a persona?

It is easier to enumerate the prerogatives that Varshavski foregoes than those he claims. With the exception of the open letter discussed earlier, Varshavski never speaks in his own voice; even there, the first-person plural predominated. Varshavski's *mir* [we], however, is not simply the editorial "we" favored generally, though not entirely consistently, in the *Forverts*. It is, rather, more of a pedagogical "we"– including both speaker and implied reader in the experience of whatever is being related while reserving to itself the privilege of narrative interpretation. The reader learns about Varshavski both by the choice of subject matter and, especially, by the speaker's attitude toward that subject matter. Varshavski remains entirely without personal history or individual attributes; he is the sum of his interests, attitudes and preoccupations.[14]

Varshavski was quite catholic in his fields of inquiry, and again it is easier to specify his nature by exclusionary, rather than additive, criteria. Notwithstanding the rare piece of timely interest (commissioned, one suspects, by his editors). Varshavski had virtually no interest in politics or even current events.[15] It is problematic and critically naive to seek the voice of historical authors in one or another of their fictional characters, but as diversion, at least, I would like to quote from a piece written at least three decades after the period here in question but set in the summer of 1938; in "The Yearning Heifer," a literarily untutored but enthusiastic common reader commends the Varshavski-like putative author for having avoided timeliness:

> "My God, I read you every week! I go to the village Friday especially to get the paper, and you won't believe me, but I read *A Bundle of Facts* before I even read the news. The news is all bad. Hitler this, Hitler that. He should burn like a fire, the no-good. What does he want from the Jews? Is it their fault that Germany lost the war? From just reading about it one could get a heart attack. But your facts are knowledge, science. Is it true that a fly has thousands of eyes?"[16]

With the near-exception of news and political commentary, Varshavski's nets were cast quite wide. His book reviews were opinionated but distinguished (one gets the impression that Singer chose his own objects of discussion here),[17] his articles on popular science a definite cut above the "Bundle of Facts" he so often, and disparagingly, mentions, his columns on historical events and personages particularly provocative. These latter writings merit some detailed scrutiny.

The first—and hence characterizing, as well as characteristic—cluster of articles by Varshavski dealt with important, if not always well-remembered, incidents and individuals from Jewish history. The very first of these was on Solomon Maimon, "A litvisher yid, velkher iz geven a betler, a kemfer far emes un eyner fun di greste filozofn in der velt" [A Lithuanian Jew Who was a Beggar, Fighter for the Truth, and One of the World's Great Philosophers].[18] The second such piece—one which, in critical synecdoche, will stand for its several dozen analogues— was entitled "A yidisher diktator in Drohobitsh, mit velkher s'hot gekokht gants Galitsye" [The Jewish Dictator of Drohobycz—The Rage of Galicia].[19] As in the previous chapter's section on *Der zindiker meshiekh*, I shall have to preface my discussion of "A yidisher diktator" with a bit of plot-summary:

Zalmen, a cashier of old Porets Khamintovski, robs him, is discovered, whipped, and banished. The *pritse*, who had fallen in love with Zalmen's aggressive virility, sends him billets-doux and meets with him clandestinely. After the *porets'* death, Zalmen is named *roshekool* [leader of the Jewish community] and enjoys, via the *pritse*, de factor control over the Gentile community as well. Everything—and everyone—is subject to his increasingly exploitive dictates. Meanwhile, Zalmen divides his time between his Jewish wife and children and the *pritse's* manor. Pressed nearly beyond endurance, the peasants attempt to lodge a lawsuit against Zalmen, but the *pritse* obtains an "iron letter" from King August III removing Zalmen from all but the court's direct jurisdiction. Years pass. Eventually, permission to sue is granted and the magistrate sentences Zalmen to death. Although the Jewish community had collected a huge sum of money with which to ransom their former oppressor, Zalmen purchases his freedom by converting to Catholicism and entering a monastery. His career as pentinent is a short one, however: less than a week after having been transported to the monastery, he succumbs to a mysterious illness and is buried on Church grounds.

The first of two installments does not begin with a survey of the literature on Zalmen Drohobitsher, Although a number of Varshavski's historical texts are, in fact, preceeded by short bibliographies. Nonetheless, the narrator assumes a stance altogether consonant with the recounting of data culled from earlier, more authoritative sources. The narration is colorless and singularly unengaged. Events are neither interpreted nor placed in causal juxtaposition with one another – they merely happen. Accordingly, there is no particular reason for the narrator to dwell on one event more than on any other; the pace of narration is leisurely enough, but tediously even-handed in distribution of emphasis and *Erzaehlzeit*.

The Varshavski of this installment bears little resemblance to the didactic, engaged, and often acerbic persona of the book reviews and occasional pieces bearing the same signature. (Nor, incidentally, does he recall the Bashevis of the *reportazhn* and minimalist fictions: while Bashevis was generally constrained to suppress certain narrative elements – action, access to characters' unarticulated thoughts, etc. – his central concern was character as filtered by an intrusive narrative consciousness; in contrast, the narrator of "A yidisher diktator" has been concerned not with character but with action, and he is linguistically all but invisible). Why this naively scientific dedication to event *wie es eigentlich gewesen*? Is this simply a "Bundle of Facts" dished up for a readership uncritically accepting of unprocessed data? One need not subscribe to the structuralist canon to agree with Jonathan Culler that "to naturalize a text is to bring it into relation with a type of discourse or model which is already, in some sense, natural and legible,"[20] and that this involves the reader in a process of genre-identification. Where the writer is unfamiliar and the work is without generic tag – we remember that "A yidisher diktator" was Varshavski's second appearance and that the piece lacks a subtitle – the work bears a heavier burden of self-identification. The Yiddish common reader was assuredly innocent of formal historiography and had, one assumes, to be given a fair sample of text before the appropriate model –

nonfictional reportage[21] – would consistently have been chosen. There was, moreover, the danger of misidentification of "A yidisher diktator" as one of the decidedly fictional historical novellas with which the Yiddish readership was more familiar. Singer's editors provided a helpful contextual clue, however, by placing his text not on the *romanzayt* [novel page] or in the magazine-like second section, but rather, on the news pages – that is, apposite to articles of unambiguous nonfictiveness; this was to become the characteristic, if not exclusive, location of Varshavski's historical pieces.

There was a single, if rather benign, inconsistency in the first installment: Varshavski enjoyed privileged access to the *priste's* thoughts. In other cases, we are left to extrapolate or forego knowledge of the characters' feelings. Was, for example, the *porets* merely angry with Zalmen, or did he feel betrayed by someone who enjoyed his special confidence? Was the reaction of the Jewish community to their fellow Jew's cruelty substantively different from that of the Gentile community? The answers to these questions are at once inaccessible (unless, of course, there were contemporary documents on the matter – a *pinkes* [community register] or the like) and not particularly important to a narrator more interested in event than in motivation. Nonetheless, the *priste's* precise thoughts are accessible to the narrator, even though such precision is not particularly central to the story's progress. We learn, in *erlebte Rede*, that she was taken by Zalmen's strength, courage, and *mansbilishe sheynkayt* [masculine beauty]. This is not, I believe, a lapse on Varshavski's part, but an early indication that the generic identity to which he had so meticulously laid claim was, and was supposed to be, less stable than it seemed.

The second installment of "A yidisher diktator" begins where the first left off, entirely without the section of plot-summary familiar to readers of historical fiction. Though I shall attempt to show how Varshavski loses no time in moving this installment from historical reportage to near-fiction, the chapter break – unlike those of *Der zindiker meshiekh* – serves to ameliorate, rather than emphasize, the shift in narrative prerogatives. The shift, further, is by no means abrupt: the familiar unengaged stance is carried forward; motivations, whether individual or collective, remain to be inferred from actions. On the other hand, we learn about the *pritse* from the narrator not merely what was otherwise evident from her actions (i.e. that she is in love with Zalmen), but what she had told no one (i.e. that, because of his additional sexual partners, Zalmen was failing to satisfy her physical desires). Lastly, we are even privy to those thoughts entirely unexpressed in actions; Zalmen is successfully brought to trial and "itst, az Zalmen iz arayngefaln in der nets, hot di pritse shtilerheyt, tif in harts, derlebt in im nekome" [now that Zalmen had fallen into the net, the *pritse* experienced, silently and deep within her heart, a feeling of revenge].

Varshavski is judicious with his lapses from documentary historiography. There are few further examples in the installment – but they are interesting ones. First, he reports the thoughts of a collective with quite the same casual assurance as he had those of an individual. Zalmen, we remember, dies within several days of his conversion to Christianity. "Yidn hobn, natirlekh, in dem alemen gezen gots hant" [Of course, the Jews saw God's hand in all this]. It would have been simple enough to convey this information as earlier data had been conveyed – through chronicling of the community's actions following Zalmen's death. But this would, I believe, have undermined what was precisely Varshavski's strategy – namely, the gradual introduction of narrative elements more properly belonging to fiction than to reportage.

With the waxing of narrative omniscience comes a concomitant waxing of narrative personality. Again, the shift is gradual and, especially for a piece in the *Forverts*, rather subtle. Whereas each incident had previously been accorded a similar amount of *Erzaehlzeit*, the narrator digresses for nearly two of four columns on the Jewish attitude toward the death penalty. Although ostensibly occasioned by his report of the Jewish community's fundraising activities on Zalmen's behalf, Varshavski quickly enough abandons the occasion and launches into a discussion of Jews and the death penalty *tout court*: "Der ekl un viderviln kegn toytshtrof ligt yidn, vayzt oys, in blut . . . [Jews' repulsion and antipathy toward the death penalty is, it seems, genetically determined. . . .] The issue is undeniably an important one but, in this context, a rather eccentric focus of attention. The narrator might more plausibly have been lured by a discussion of Jewish-Gentile relations – personal, communal, or religious,[22] Zalmen's presumed responsibility to his family and people in conflict with individual predilections leading away from them,[23] etc. That Varshavski digresses at all, and particularly on the relatively peripheral issue of the death penalty, tends to foreground his role as mediating personality while undermining the piece's documentary status.

The concluding paragraph accelerates and culminates this movement away from uninterpretive historiography. After a geometric pattern of asterisks, the text concludes as follows:

> Yede geshikhte hot ir moral. Un oykh fun der geshikhte mit Zalmen Drohobitsher ken men epes lernen. Men ken derfun aroyslernen, as makht iz nit eybik, un az di yenike vos nitsn oys zeyer makht tsum shlekhtn, muzn frier oder shpeter faln. Zalmen iz, eygntlekh, geven a diktator, khotsh fun kleynem farnem, un oykh zahn biterer sof iz geven der zelber, vos es hobn frier oder shpeter, ale diktatorn, kleyne oder groyse. . . .
>
> [Every story has its moral. And one can learn something from the story of Zalmen of Drohobycz as well. One can draw the conclusion that power is not eternal, and that those who use their power for ill must, sooner or later, fall. Zalmen was, in fact a dictator, though of modest proportions, and his bitter end, too, was the same as comes, sooner later, to all dictators, great or small.]

Singer plays on the word *geshikhte*, which (as its German cognate) may mean both "story" and "history." On the one hand, the word is not an unequivocal *daytshmerizm* [stylistically substandard borrowing from New High German][24] – Weinreich cites it without cautionary siglum in his *Dictionary*.[25] On the other hand, *geshikhte* has few reverberations in Yiddish: Stutchkoff does list *geshikhte* in his *Oytser* in both of its meanings,[26] but one is struck by the paucity of compounds and derivatives of which it is an element: *geshikhte* is "history," but *historish*, not **geshikhtlekh*, is "historical"; *historiker*, not **geshikhtler*, is "historian"; moreover, *geshikhte* generates not a single derivative in its meaning of "story," as compared with twelve for *mayse* [story, tale].[27] Nor, incidentally, did Singer ever use *geshikhte* as generic tag to one of his writings under whatever pseudonym. The term was, then, unmarked and available for generic definition or, as here, play.

Singer has, as we have seen, shaded nonfictional historical reportage into near-fiction. The process has been gradual; its later stages may clash ontologically with its earlier ones, but stylistically the metamorphosis is smooth. It is unlikely that a reader would have noted the change, though he or she surely would have made the appropriate modifications in naturalizing the text. There is, however, a final movement in the reverse direction – one which recasts the text as nonfiction, but as nonfiction of a very different sort. This final reversal is, I suspect, as unanticipated as the *kneytsh* [plot reversal; lit., twist] at the end of a short story by Perets; it inheres, however, not within the text, but in the relationship between the text and those with which it is surrounded. Bracketing "A yidisher diktator" in the news pages of the *Forverts* are reports on the contemporary dictatorships of Hitler in Germany, Mussolini in Italy, Franco in Spain, Goga in Romania, Imredy in Hungary, Stalin in the Soviet Union. In this context, Varshavski's assertion that all dictators must sooner or later fall is of the most urgent nonfictional import. The text, then, is triply determined – as nonfictional historiography, as historical fiction, and as nonfictional commentary on current political events. This is an empressive performance indeed, and one the sophistication of which quite justifies the year of inactivity which preceded it.

Though not all of Varshavski's contributions to the *Forverts* of the 1940's were as carefully crafted as "A yidisher diktator," Singer is surely mistaken in dismissing them as hackwork.[28] Indeed, hackwork generally implies furious production of paid-by-the-word ephemera, whereas, in fact, Singer's total production in these years was both modest and consistent – a handful of articles or book reviews signed Bashevis in the *Tsukunft* or a similar literary-intellectual journal,[29] and approximately one piece a week in the *Forverts* signed Varshavski. To be sure, this represents a sharp rise over the sporadic production of earlier years, but is – to use the medical metaphor of which Singer is so fond – rather a sign of authorial well-being than of illness.[30]

Thematically, Varshavski's writings were eclectic in the extreme; a contemporary reader would likely have been as engaged in anticipating the topic of the next week's article as in reading the article itself: an historical piece might, without transition, be followed by one on folk customs, literary movements,

romance in the animal kingdom, or the pernicious effects of med-
dling relatives on otherwise sound marriages.[31] In each case,
however, the structure would be familiar: the narrator begins by
stating a general problem or concern, often citing bibliographical
sources; he moves into a rather impersonal illustrative example;
in the course of exposition he asserts narrative prerogatives which
move the incident from reportage toward fiction; he concludes
with the *nimshl* and *muser-haskl* [roughly: moral] of traditional
Jewish folk narration.[32] To have developed an approach which
enlists such diverse subject matter in the service of a single narrative strategy is itself a remarkable achievement.

Bashevis' approach to writing fiction as reportage was, as we
have seen, inherently unstable: each successive text was more
radically undermining of generic norms; the process ended with
chaotic texts and, ultimately, with a silent persona. Varshavski's
approach to writing reportage as fiction was, in contrast, unusually stable: texts of the most diverse content were cut to the
measure of a rhetorically useful if predictable formula; the only
inherent limits to this process were Singer-Varshavski's literary
productivity and the amount of space made available by the
Forverts. When, in 1942, Singer was offered the opportunity of
doubling his production – one wonders whether his salary was
ommensurately adjusted – it is not surprising that he should have
seized the opportunity in mid-week.

It would, however, have been unseemly for the *Forverts* to
go to print with double the number of articles by a staff writer
of less than stellar reputation.[33] Whether or not the readership
would have noticed is rather beside the point; Varshavski's fellows
at 175 East Broadway would surely not have welcomed the
change. A new pseudonym was called for – one a great deal more
opaque than the previous two. On 21 June 1942, Singer signed
his first piece D. Segal.[34] Not until 1972, in Leonard Prager's *Encyclopedia Judaica* article on Singer, did the anglophone world learn
the identity of the putative author of, between 1942 and 1951
alone (i.e., Segal's first decade in print), some 299 pieces in the
Forverts.[35] (By contrast, Varshavski published 359 pieces during
the same period, and Bashevis only 15.)[36] More surprisingly,
however, the Yiddish literary world also remained generally ignorant of Segal's identity, though the name surely must have been
recognized as a pseudonym.[37] To have kept one's pseudonym con-

fidential for nearly four decades in a society of literary cafés and cafeterias, private parties and public lectures is itself worthy of a short story in the *Forverts*.[38]

At the outset, there was little to differentiate Segal's oeuvre from Varshavski's. Both wrote on the most diverse topics, and in much the same voice. Gradually, though Segal assumed authorship of those pieces of a more familial, personal, or unguardedly sexual nature. While Varshavski, in 1943, could still publish a column on "Geburt-kontrol—A frage nit bloyz farn privatn lebn nor oykh far der politik fun felker un regirungen" [Birth Control: More than a Private Matter—One that Touches the Politics of States and Peoples][39] only Segal, in 1945, could risk one on "Mener vos vern oyf di eltere yorn romantish" [Men Who Turn Romantic in Old Age].[40] Understandably enough, these often provoked correspondence from readers; letters were welcomed, for they, like latter-day viewers' letters to television programs or networks, were tangible evidence of an audience. Indeed, Varshavski had more than once solicited reader response to his evocations of Jewish folk observances; he invited readers to submit recalled proverbs and witticisms, holiday customs and given names.[41] Although these columns were demonstrably popular with the readership[42] (and they relieved Singer from much of the burden of turning out what were now two weekly columns), Varshavski was necessarily limited as a correspondent: disgruntled correspondents could seek redress, by mail or in person, from a decidedly real Isaac Singer;[43] moreover, excessive attention to the subject matter of his contributions deflected attention from their ultimate function as reportage-made-fiction.

Segal could better bear these distractons. First, reader response was evidence of independent interest in his pieces. Second, he was utterly inaccessible, inhering, as he did, solely within the texts of which he was putative author; the most determined would-be colloquant could find no one answering to Segal's name anywhere this side of print-on-paper. Finally, as is both typical of Singer and evidence of his artistic vigor, he discovered in this situation an important new approach to the writing of reportage as fiction.

Typical of Segal's more tentative efforts to pursue strategies distinct from Varshavski's was a series of articles beginning with the *geshikhte* [story, history] of an immigrant Jew who, almost without effort and nearly against his will, winds up a millionaire.[44] He is afraid that his newly-obtained wealth will estrange him from his family and from the only way of life he finds congenial.[45] Unlike other Segal pieces, there is no indication in the text how the author learned of the millionair's quandary, but the narrator's tone and well-informed exposition invites the reader to naturalize the text as reportage. The narrator's status as chronicler is further emphasized by his disinclination to offer advice or commentary at the piece's rather abrupt conclusion. Like Varshavski, then Segal presumes the literal historicity of his account; unlike Varshavski, he declines overtly to adopt the conventions of fictional closure.

Nonetheless, several of Segal's narrative prerogatives more properly recall those of fictional narrators than those of reporters. One is struck, for example, by the absence of documentary preliminaries which would explain how the narrator obtained reliable information about his millionaire; without these, the piece remains midway between fiction and reportage. Be that as it may, the piece generated a flood of replies from readers, always ready to dispose of (or garner for themselves) another's fortune.[46] It is, of course, impossible to determine how many of these replies were genuine; all were certainly represented as such. I would be surprised were they all Segal-written (or, for that matter, all genuine). Insofar as Segal's readers also wondered about the authenticity of these replies, distinctions between fiction and reportage were further – and profitably – blurred.[47]
Segal's appropriation of a format initially developed by Varshavski (and, for the most part, ignored by other *Forverts* writers) might – it is impossible to tell – have served to link the two in the eyes of their readership. At all events, it has given us an opportunity to examine an interesting variation of Singer's general practice of exploiting inherited genres: here one pseudonymous persona begins his career by settling scores with the pseudonymous persona that preceded him. At the same time, however, Segal was developing other, more radical means of shading reportage into fiction.

II

Initially, then, Segal's approach and subject matter both resembled those of Varshavski. Over time, however, Segal's personal, familial, and sexual preoccupations began to force out – not completely, but predominantly – other interests, which were gradually ceded to Varshavski. Conversely, Varshavski's writings became increasingly intellectual, speculative, and text-oriented. Withal, it is important to realize that Segal's writings laid no less rigorous a claim to absolute veracity than did Varshavski's. Indeed, the former's pieces were almost always placed in apposition to items of hard news, in contrast to Varshavski's customary location on the op-ed pages. Of the two Segal columns I discuss below, one adjoins a bylined article on "Der militarisher shnayder Bornshteyn, velkher hot geshikt zayne finf zin in milkhome" [Bornstein, Tailor to the Military, Who Sent His Five Sons to War],[48] the other an unsigned news dispatch from Palestine, "Sovetrussland vet zikh nit mishn in der frage fun emigratsye keyn Erets-yisroel" [Soviet Russia Won't Interfere with Jewish Emigration to Palestine].[49]

One would expect Segal to exploit these contextual markers to assert the literal historicity of the incidents he reports, if only to protect himself from charges of salacious fictionalizing. This is especially crucial, since – in contrast to Varshavski's allusions to events in Jewish history already known, however sketchily, by at least a portion of the readership – the stuff of Segal's pieces is typically contemporary, private, and hence difficult to verify independently. And, in fact, he does assert their veracity, but in ways quite different from Varshavski. The latter, we may remember, cites historical sources – sometimes rather generally, often by precise title. Segal, on the other hand, most frequently cites the testimony of friends and trusted colleagues. In "Er hot zikh getrofn mit zayn 'geshtorbener' gelibter" [He Met His "Dead" Lover],[50] for example, Segal introduces a discussion of lovers and spouses reunited after the displacements of the Second World War by citing the source of the anecdote which, ostensibly, moved him to write on the topic:

Der shrayber fun di shures aleyn hot zikh shoyn getrofn mit
etlekhe fraynd, velkhe er not gehaltn far toyt. Eyn mol iz
aryngekumen in redaktsye zayner a yugnt-khaver, vegn velkhn
er iz zikher geven, az er iz shoyn lang oyf der velt nishto.
[The author of these lines himself has already encountered a
number of friends whom he had thought dead. Once one of his
childhood friends whom he had been certain was no longer in
this world came into the editorial offices.]

His friend's unexpected visit is only the merest pretext for a series
of associationally-linked anecdotes of increasing emotional inten-
sity: former lovers meet on the streets of New York, in a D.P. camp,
at the very gates of a newly-liberated concentration camp. Like
Varshavski, Segal moves from description to imaginative
recreation:

Azoyne bagegenishn . . . kumen for . . . merkvirdik shtil. Der man
tut a gey tsu tsu der froy un ruft on ir nomen. Er iz nisht in gantsn
zikher. Efsher makht er a toes? Di froy kukt zikh um un tut a
laykhtn oysgeshrey, oder efsher dos oykh nisht.
[Such meetings . . . come about . . . remarkably quietly. The man
takes a step toward the woman and calls her by name. He is not
entirely certain. Perhaps he's making a mistake. The woman looks
around and cries out softly, or perhaps not even that.]

Segal's caution in describing this scene (". . . or perhaps not even
that") works both to obscure and to highlight its status as fiction;
he is striving for accuracy in a narrative which, since it is entirely
hypothetical, does not a priori admit of reportorial exactitude.
The visitor to the editorial offices, whose appearance occasioned
these anecdotes and whose ostensible extratextual existence
tempers their fictiveness, is, by the way, never returned to in the
course of the piece.

Like Varshavski, Segal seeks to derive a moral or morals from
his history. These are announced in the latter part of a serpentine subtitle: "Di psikhologishe shverikaytn zikh tsutsupasn tsu
der virklekhkayt.—Yesurim endern mentshn nit azoy fil vi men
gleybt" [The Psychological Difficulties of Adjusting to Reality; Suffering Does Not Change People as Much as One Might Think].[51]

In a sense, then, the entire chain of anecdotes has been preparation for a number of general statements in Segal's own voice, first on applied psychology and then on practical ethics (how one should speak with Holocaust victims; how probing one's questioning may legitimately be).

Formally, Segal's strategy mirrors that of Varshavski, at least in a great number of instances: both recount events which have, or are alleged to have, actually taken place; both assume prerogatives in the course of the narratives which more properly belong to fictional narrators; both conclude their accounts with a moral, which moral is, with retrospective logic, the piece's raison d'être. Substantively, however, there is a crucial set of differences between the two personas' production – one which provides more than adequate literary justification for Singer's practical decision to invent D. Segal. These differences all bear on the real-world authenticity of the events chronicled.

Briefly, Segal destabilizes the generic identity of his pieces by placing in question the documentary authenticity of the embedded incidents. Surveying Segal's production for a single year – 1945 – we find that he has depicted a reasonable number of social situations which, if a bit luridly headlined, are believable enough. These would include "Er gloybt in zayn vayb khotsh ale faktn zaynen kegn ir" [Believes in His Wife Even Though Facts Are Stacked Against Her],[52] and "Di tokhter hot zikh ayngeredt az zi iz an aktrise" [Daughter Persuades Herself She's an Actress].[53] On the other hand, other situations would strain the credulity of the most devoted "Bintl Briv" reader –"Ir khosn hot zikh farlibt in ir mame" [Her Fiancé Fell in Love with Her Mother][54] or "Er hot zikh geget mit zayn froy un zi genumen far [a] gelibter" [Divorced His Wife and Took Her as Lover],[55] for example. Furthermore, Segal's sources for these incidents are rather sketchily cited. In "Er hot zikh getrofn mit zayn 'geshtorbener' gelibter" [He Met His "Dead" Lover], for example, only the first of several associationally-linked anecdotes (the childhood friend's unexpected appearance at the *Forverts* office) is located by speaker and narrative occasion; later anecdotes are introduced by a transitional sentence or phrase which does not, except perhaps by implication, claim historicity: "In fil faln iz aza bagegenish farbundn mit groyse komplikatsyes" [In many cases such a meeting brings great complications]. This reportorial nonspecificity reaches its logical conclusion in an otherwise undocumented "Ober ot iz an ander fal" [But here is another case].[56]

Finally, even the least credible of Varshavski's historical curiosia derives its authority as nonfictional historiography from printed sources, rather than personal communication. Quite aside from the actual existence or nonexistence of these sources (most of Varshavski's citations appear to be accurate, though their accuracy is less important than their presence), the printed word weighs very differently than does its spoken counterpart. John Ellis makes a complementary point in his chapter on "The Relevant Context of a Literary Text" when he notes that "over and over again we meet the notion that the valued texts are written in an older form of the language, so that an older form comes to have a function in the contemporary language of being the language of the sacred and venerable texts."[57] I certainly do not suggest that Varshavski writes in, say, Middle Yiddish (or, to preserve the parallel to Latin or Old Church Slavonic, classical Hebrew), but both the fact that his ostensible source texts are in Hebrew or older Yiddish and that Varshavski's own rather formal Yiddish has a substantially greater admixture of words from the Hebrew-Aramaic element lend his texts greater authority than Segal's, whose sources are purportedly oral and whose own lexical proclivities tend definitely toward the colloquially Yinglish — *trobl, vakeyshon, elimoni, kontri, honimun, plezhur*.

It is tempting, particularly in light of the low-browedness of these pieces and the unsophistication of what one assumes to have been their primary readership, to regard Segal as a less conscientious Varshavski, much as Singer has characterized Varshavski as a less conscientious Bashevis. But, in fact, rather the opposite is true. With his identity more thoroughly protected, Segal was able to undertake experiments no longer possible for Varshavski. One such experiment is a remarkable piece entitled "Er hot forgeshtelt zayn gelibte als zayn shvester" [He Introduced His Lover as His Sister].[58] Cast in the standard Segalesque mode, it purports to tell the true story of a man who lived with a sexually satisfying but otherwise somewhat coarse lover; the man travels to Europe, brings home an intelligent, gentle but maddeningly naive young wife. After a time, he introduces his now-reclaimed lover as his sister from San Francisco. (He, in fact, has a sister, still resident in San Francisco and not inclined toward correspondence.) He divides his attentions between wife and "sister"– happily, and for years. Only the unheralded arrival of a niece from San Francisco disturbs the domestic peace. The situation ends in chaos – a wife suing for divorce after her nervous breakdown, a lover pressing for marriage, a flustered young woman returning to San Francisco, a man immobilized in the face of mounting disaster.

The frame of "Er hot forgeshtelt zayn gelibte" is a bit atypical: rather than citing his source for these events (a friend, colleague, random visitor to the editorial offices, or the like), Segal prefaces his narrative with a rather extensive retelling of the biblical account of how Abraham persuades Sarah to masquerade as his sister in Egypt, and with a briefer allusion to a similar account involving Isaac and Rebecca. It is as if Segal attempts to compensate for his lack of real-world anchoring of at least the initial anecdote (we have already seen how, in other pieces, diverse anecdotes may be strung together associationally without further source citations) by allusion to a canonized text the literal historicity of which no professing Jew could deny. This gambit is, of course, a logically defective invocation of biblical authority: proving that similar events had once – actually, twice – before taken place does not speak to the veracity of a specific set of later events but only, at most, to their potential verisimilitude; a single eye-witness would be more to the point here than the entire book of Genesis. The gambit is, moreover, rhetorically defective: the *Forverts,* an aggressively secularist newspaper hostile to all but the folkloristic aspects of Jewish tradition, enjoyed a readership more likely to be put off than persuaded by allusion to the Hebrew Scriptures.[59] (Darwin or Marx would have been quite another matter.)

The piece concludes with the generically-mandated moral, derived by the narrator from the events just chronicled; to this is appended a coda-like return to the opening biblical conceit:

Di moral fun der geshikhte iz: Ershtns, shtelt nit for ayer gelibte als ayer "shvester". Tsveytns, hot nit khasene biz vanen ir hot nit gesetelt mit ayer frierdiker gelibter. Dritns, oyb ir hot a shvester

in San-frantsisko un zi hot a tokhter, dervart yedn tog, az zi vet
araynfaln tsu aykh vi a blits un aykh makhn trobl, saydn ayer
gevisn iz reyn. . . . Dos vos es iz gelungen Avrom avinun in Mits-
rayim, vet aykh nit gelingen in Bruklin. . . .

[The moral of this story is: First, don't introduce your lover as your
"sister." Second, don't get married until you've settled things with
your lover. Third, if you have a sister in San Francisco and she
has a daughter, expect her to land in your home like a bolt from
the blue and make trouble, unless your conscience is clean. . . .
What Abraham pulled off in Egypt you won't get away with in
Brooklyn.]

The ironic intent of Segal's conclusion is as unmistable as it is
delightful. It is clear that something is being undermined, and
worth the effort to sort out exactly what.

First, the Hebrew Scriptures are denied either predictive or
exemplary value, though the historicity of their accounts
themselves is not called into question. (*That* might have been
incautious even writing for a *Forverts* readership, and would not,
incidentally, have reflected Singer's own views; moreover, a
demonstration of the inappropriateness of biblical precedent to
contemporary affairs is purposeless unless both vehicle and tenor
are accorded some measure of credibility.) Second, the predictable closure of both Varshavski's and Segal's *geshikhtes* is here
reduced to a formal, rather than an ethical, exigency. This piece
ends with a moral because, generically, it must – quite a displace-
ment from the didactic motivation of "A yidisher diktator"'s
closure: "fun der geshikhte . . . ken men epes lernen" [one can
learn something from this story]. After nearly a half-dozen years
of taking itself seriously, the genre engages in a bit of Jakobso-
nian *obnazenie priëma* [laying bare of the device].[60] Segal has, as
we have seen, raised successive doubts first about the source of
"Er hot forgeshtelt zayn gelibte," then about the predictive value
of biblical analysis, and lastly about the moral one might properly extrapolate from his text. The latter two layings-bare undermine generic constraints in these pieces without, however,
endangering their ontological status, which is, in all events,
predicated upon an interplay of historical documentary with
imaginative narrative intervention. If Varshavski continues to

believe that one can learn from history while Segal comes to question the applicability of past events to present conduct, neither is willing to let historical data speak for itself or to refrain from asserting prerogatives appropriate only to narrators of fictions. In this respect, both engage in writing reportage as fiction.

Segal's apparent disinclination to cite his sources, on the other hand, poses a more fundamental threat to the genre's integrity. By undermining the embedded events' claim to literal historicity, Segal moots the underlying rhetorical strategy: one cannot fictioalize that which is already fictional. Lest his readers suspend disbelief too readily, Segal interrupts his narrative with an oddly placed and phrased subtitle. Articles in the *Forverts* are, as a rule, not subdivided into sections with boldface dividers, as is customary in the English-language press. Yiddish newspaper articles are rarely subdivided, but frequently are prefaced by a lengthy teaser amplifying the main headline; this may be located adjacent and to the left of the headline, underneath it and extending over as many columns as the headline itself (usually three one-and-three-quarter-inch columns), or, in boldface, preceding the first column's text proper. By contrast, Segal's teaser appears at the head of the second column, separated from the headline by a split double rule and from the text by a column-wide single rule; moreover, its layout – twenty-six words spread over nine descending lines of type – makes it all but impossible to scan. One could hardly imagine a less eye-catching position.[61] Style abets format: the teaser begins dully enough to deter all but the most intrepid reader. In transcribed near-facsimile, it reads as follows:

A drame, vos iz geven
farbundn mit 3 shtet:
Varshe, Nyu-york, San-
frantsikso.– Di plime-
nitse kumt un tseshtert
dem sholem-baysis.– A
hekhst-shpanende
"emese" geshikhte, frish
  oysgetrakht.
[A Drama Involv-

ing Three Cities:
Warsaw, New York, San
Francisco.—His Niece
Comes and Disrupts
The Domestic Harmony. A
Highly Suspenseful
"True" Story, Freshly
    Thought Up.]

Fun D. Segal
[By D. Segal]

-----------------1¾"-----------------

If it is slow to gather momentum, the subtitle certainly ends with a *kneytsh*.

Clearly, then, Segal's earlier and less broad hints that the stuff of his narratives might not be utterly historical were neither lapses nor indiscretions. As he had earlier called into question the value of moving reportage toward fiction, he here calls into question the utility of positing a nonfictional underlying incident. "Er hot forgeshtelt zayn gelibte" is, hence, fiction as reportage as fiction—a generic and ontological mishmash, but one which serves Singer's ends exceedingly well. If, as I have argued, Singer's underlying strategy and ultimate goal is the blurring of distinctions between the fictional and the historical, he could hardly have done a better job than in these pieces the existence and authorship of which he is now so reluctant to acknowledge. They are, I believe, among Singer's major achievements.

III

We have seen how Varshavski and Segal pursued the same general strategy of writing reportage as fiction, but with markedly different tempers. Throughout the decade and well into the 1950s, Varshavski's prose remained more polished, his narrative voice more ponderous, his interests more earnest and catholic than Segal's. On the other hand, Varshavski's diverse interests were presented with formulaic regularity; there was little literary growth – though much of intellectual merit – between Varshavski's initial appearance in 1939 and the first of the autobiographical memoirs some dozen years later.[62]

By contrast, Segal continued to specialize in breezily (perhaps also hastily) written domestic melodrama. But just as Varshavski's wide range of topics was undercut by a sameness in execution, Segal's thematic predictability was enlivened both by the juiciness of the situations he depicted and, especially, by a continuing play-ing off in his pieces of fiction against reportage. This was a public game in which the readers were invited – indeed compelled – to participate. As such, the clues had to be rather unmistakable – the "'emese geshikhte', frish oysgetrakht," for example. Before sum-ming up Segal's accomplishments in particular and this second phase of Singer's productive career in general, I would like to ex-amine at some length another of Segal's pieces in which the readers' role was yet more specific.

"A froy hot fartroyt dem redaktor a vikhtikn sod" [Woman Trusts Editor with Important Secret][63] begins as follows:

> A lezer iz arayngekumen in redaktsye. . . . Zi hot gezogt, az zi muz zen dem redaktor. Zi darf fregn an eytse vegn zeyer a vikhtikn inyen. Der redaktor, vos farnemt zikh mit azelkhe zakhn, hot zi aryangebetn tsu zikh in tsimer. . . . Zi hot dertseyln [sic] a groysn sod.
>
> [A reader entered the editorial offices. . . . She said she had to speak with the editor. She had to ask for his advice about a very important matter. . . . The editor who takes care of such things invited her into his office. . . . She told (him) a big secret.]

The piece continues with a direct quotation from the visitor. Clearly, then, Segal was himself "the editor who takes care of such things." The subtitle summarizes the mother's account adequately: "Ir tokhter firt a libe mit a farheyratn man. – Er hot a vayb mit tsvey kinder. – Er hot lib zeyer tokhter, ober er vil nit tsebrekhn di heym. – Di tokhter hot sholem gemakht mit der lage. – A konflikt tsvishn di eltern" [Her Daughter Is Having an Affair with a Married Man; He Has a Wife And Two Children; He Loves Their Daughter but Doesn't Want to Break Up His Home; The Daughter Has Made Her Peace with the Situation; A Conflict Between the

Parents]. The text proper presents more details in somewhat more literary style, but the facts are, essentially, conveyed in the subtitle. Should, the mother wishes to know, the parents attempt to separate their thirty-year-old daughter from her lover or acquiesce to a situation nonproductive of grandchildren? The mother favors intervention, the father benign neglect. Segal declines to answer the mother, either in the interview or in his column: "Es iz nisht lzykht tsu entfern oyf aza sort frage" [It isn't easy to reply to such a question]; rather, he urges his readers to submit their answers: "Ez iz a problem, vos rirt on toyznter mentshn. Alzo, mir vartn oyf ayere briv" [It's a problem which touches thousands of persons. So we're awaiting your letters]; in a later appeal for responses, he all but states that it is his readers' moral obligation to reply: "Es rirt on zeyer fil mentshn, un es hot tsu ton mit der alter frage vegn libe un "moral" [It touches very many people, and it has to do with the old question of love and morality].[64]

Two years after he revealed the source of at least one of his stories as his own imagination, and made light of the genre's ability to produce moral answers even to incidents of unquestioned historicity, Segal is urging his readers to respond. Unlike Varshavski, who gave detailed instructions regarding the mechanics of replying to *Forverts* queries (readers were to write legibly, spell correctly, enlist competent help if their writing abilities were limited, keep replies concise).[65] Segal seems anxious to receive replies of any sort: he solicits them in two successive columns, despite his report in the latter that replies already far exceed space available for their publication. And, though Segal's tone remains characteristically breezy, he appears to take the issue very seriously indeed. To what are we to ascribe this new-found earnestness?

Segal was, I believe, still in the business of blurring the distinctions between fiction and reportage, but his strategy in these reader-response columns was quite different from that in the fictionalized chronicles. There, as we have seen, it suited his purpose to undermine the historicity of reported events. By contrast, here it is important to establish the readers' credence in the situation portrayed: from this base line of accepted historicity, Segal was to try his hand at a set of different, though no less extreme, strategies to destabilize the texts' generic identity. We see, incidentally, how Segal exploits generic norms established by Varshavski, whose own and whose readers' reports on festival observances and the like derive their authority as history both from the sacred texts which mandate the festivals and from collective popular memory which recalls how they were observed.

In one respect, at least, Segal even exceeded Varshavski in the matter of documentation: Varshavski had summarized what were said to have been readers' replies to his queries — infrequently in loose paraphrase, more frequently in an edited overview which merged the contributions of specific correspondents. These informants were never named or otherwise identified (save, on occasion, to indicate the area of Eastern Europe for which they claimed expertise); there is no particular reason to assume their extratextual existence, especially in light of the altogether impersonal — though not necessarily ethnographically uninteresting — nature of their reports. Segal, on the other hand, gives the name and exact street address of his respondents — Philip Kuper of 315 Hopkins Avenue, Brooklyn; Lina Kaplan of 225 East 91st Street, Brooklyn; Maks Lubart of 26 South Richard Street, Ventnor City, New Jersey; there are some twenty-seven of these in the course of two articles. There is, of course, no guarantee that Segal did not invent these correspondents for the occasion, but a reader is certainly dissuaded from suspecting this. Moreover, a sprinkling of respondents make use of incomplete or pseudonymous signatures; these too, are duly recorded by the columnist —"Sem Yolov (keyn adres hot der lezer nit ongegeben [the reader gave no address])" or "a lezer, vos shraybt zikh unter Sh. B." [a reader who signs him/herself Sh. B.] are two examples. One suspects that more than one irate *Forverts* reader would have stormed the nonfictional editorial offices had these eminently verifiable respondents' names proven to have been imaginary. Why, then, this atypical documentary specificity?

The readers' responses were, I suggest, provided to lend at least initial credibility to an article by one Menakhem Podolyer which appeared in the *Forverts* for 18 December 1947 — three days after Segal's publication of the first column in this series. Podolyer's article is remarkable in its naivete, unintended humor, and unrestrained *khutspe*; as we shall see, it is remarkable in other, more sophisticated ways as well. It is entitled "Vi eltern darfn handlen ven zeyer tokhter firt a libe mit a farheyratn man" [How Parents Should Act When Their Daughter Has an Affair with a Married Man].[66] Podolyer begins by asserting his "legal" right to reply to Segal—he is, after all, a reader of the *Forverts* and, as such, entitled to accept Segal's invitation, as well as being a professional and regularly-published columnist, which confers to right of reply in an article of his own. The tone and exact text are important:

> In zayn artikl . . . hot mayn fraynd un kolege D. Segal dertseylt a geshikhte. . . . Nu, bin ikh oykh a lezer un ikh vil oykh oysdrukn mayn meynung. Ikh hob, gloyb ikh, a rekht deroyf, vayl punkt vi mayn kolege D. Segal, bin ikh oykh a boki in familyen-ongeleygnhaytn un ikh hob shoyn a hipsh bisl geshribn vegn azelkhe inyonim, vos m'endikt geveyntlekh dermit, az in azelkhe faln iz zeyer shver yenem tsu gebn an eytse, vayl di problem iz zeyer a shvere.
> [My friend and colleague, D. Segal, told a story in his article. . . . Well, I'm also a reader and want to express my opinion. I have, I believe, a right to do so, because just like my colleague D. Segal, I'm also an expert in family matters and I've already written quite a bit about those cases where one concludes that it's very difficult to give the person any advice because the problem's a very difficult one.] (p. 2)

Podolyer continues by complaining of Segal's alleged support of the daughter's misadventures, dismissing her as a "beheyme" [beast]. He recommends an enforced vacation in Florida, where, he assures us, she is certain to meet an eligible young man—Jewish, of course. Podolyer views this as a cautionary tale about overindulgent parents and overly-sympathetic newspaper columnists.

Podolyer's piece is, in the main, deliciously naive: he assumes that a vacation will "cure" the young woman of a commitment which has endured for years and with the inherent limitations of which both participants have made their peace. Segal's article had revealed quite a bit about the participants' characters; the quandry arose because father, mother, daughter, and lover were all decent people—it was only their desires and values which were irreconcilable. In fact, the mother had even met clandestinely with her daugher's lover, and was surprised to leave thinking rather highly of him.[67] Yet Podolyer's disdain for the lot was barely disguised, his dislike for the daughter positively virulent. It is not merely that his values are so injudiciously expressed which destroys Podolyer's credibility; one is entitled to strong opinions in such matters. Rather, his perceptions are at odds with the facts of the situation as they were reported – and as one might fairly assume them to be. His obtuseness in matters of fact discredits, rhetorically if not logically, his conclusions in matters of nonempirical judgment.

Moreover, Podolyer *sounds* unlike a professional writer. Yiddish journalistic style in general, and *Forverts* usage in particular, discourage writing in the first-person singular; we have seen how even as casual a writer as Segal avoids this voice. Podolyer, on the other hand, is unprofessionally conversational in his use of the first-person singular; I have already cited two consecutive sentences with seven first-person pronouns. His expostulations cast him more as fictional visitor to the editorial offices than as employee there: "Nu, bin ikh oykh a lezer" [Well, I'm also a reader]; "Bin ikh oykh a boki" [I'm also an expert]. I am, in fact, persuaded that Podolyer was entirely fictitious: no such signature appears on articles in the *Forverts* (or, insofar as I have been able to determine, anywhere else in the Yiddish press) for the two years preceding this article; no such name is registered in the YIVO or Library of Congress catalogues, or in the appropriate volumes of the authoritative *Leksikon fun der nayer yidisher literatur* [Lexicon of Modern Yiddish Literature];[68] a senior colleague who was and remains active in Yiddish cultural circles has also never heard the name, whether as pseudonym or orthonym. Podolyer's existence is, in short, a sham – and one recognizable as such by even a marginally astute reader. Segal sought, then, such an unusual measure of documented historicity in his solicitation and citation of reader response with the end of slipping in an obvious fictional ringer. Podolyer's presence is as jarring as that of Bugs Bunny in a commercial featuring live actors in an unlikely, but naturalistically-filmed, setting: by violating generic norms, he destroys any pre-existing suspension of disbelief in a situation of asserted, but not incontrovertible, literal historicity. If Podolyer is unreal, one is justified in inquiring after the reality of Philip Kuper of Hopkins Avenue.

Had Singer's newest pseudonymous persona done no more than destabilize the ontology of Segal's texts both more gracefully and more thoroughly than Singer had theretofore been able to achieve, it would have been accomplishment enough. But the substance, as well as the narration, of Podolyer's column bears examination.[69] Though Podolyer objects to the young woman's behavior on intrinsic grounds, he reserves much of his emotional investment for a curiously anachronistic denunciation of the power of literature to influence readers' lives; the young woman was led astray, he tells us, by an over-avid consumption of *bikhlekh* [books, in the contemptuous diminutive]:[70]

> In der emesn handlt zikh do . . . vegn a meydl, vos hot zikh avade ongeleynt mit azelkhe bikhlekh, vos zi hot nit gedarft leyenen, un itst lebt zi loytn muster fun epes a bikhl, vos zi hot shlekht far-shtanen. . . . Dos iz a meydl, vos "lebt literatur," oyb m'ken zikh azoy oysdrukn. Dos heyst, zi firt zikh azoy az onshtot tsu zayn a lebediker mentsh, vos iz eng farbundn mit der virklekhkayt, mit dem lebn klept zi fun zikh oys epes a min stroyene heldin, vos past zikh arayn in ir tsedreyter fantazye . . . [In point of fact this is the case of a girl who filled her mind with the kind of books she should not have read, and now is patterning her life after a book which she has misunderstood. . . . This is a girl who is "liv-ing literature," if I may be permitted the expression. That is, instead of acting like a living being intimately bound to reality, to life, she's turned herself into a cardboard heroine suited to her fantasies.]

It is, one assumes, possible to influence proverbial impres-sionable young minds by the choice of books with which they are permitted to come into contact (though not, I suspect, to the extent feared by censoring adults). One is struck less by the implausibility of Podolyer's comments, however, than by their utter inapplicability to the case at hand: this *meydl* is a thirty-year-old woman with advanced education and responsible employment. Moreover, Segal's column devotes barely four sentences in midparagraph to her youthful reading habits and none at all to her current proclivities; the complete discussion is as follows:

> Der foter hot derloybt zayn tokhter zol leyenen vosere bikher zi vil nor, un zi hot fri ongehoybn tsu leyenen romanen un alerlay

andere verk, vos bahandlen di problemen fun man un froy. Dos meydl hot vifl mol zikh oysgedrukt, az zi vet nisht khasene hobn saydn zi vet zayn farlibt in dem man mit layb un lebn. Di eltern hobn mit ir ayngeshtimt. Gevis darf zayn azoy. [The father permitted his daughter to read whatever books she wanted to, and she began early to read novels which dealt with the problems of men and women. The girl stated many times that she would only marry a man with whom she was utterly in love. Her parents agreed with her. Certainly that's the way things should be.]

Not only do her (fallible) parents agree with their daughter; the (less fallible and characteristically laconic) narrator does as well. Indeed, the piece derives much of its poignancy precisely from the irreconcilability of individually unimpeachable values.

Though we do not know enough about Menakem Podolyer to divine the reasons for his brilliantly misdirected attack on imaginative literature, Singer's motives are accessible enough. First, of course, the more outrageous Podolyer's opinions seem, the more likely the reader is to recognize him as a fictional character; and this, in turn, is essential for correct apprehension of his column. More interestingly, Podolyer recalls and embodies a premodern fear of fiction antedating the rise of maskilic popular literature. While Sholom Aleichem condemns the deleterious effects of nonrealistic fiction on one's aesthetic sensibilities without positing pernicious effects on one's extraliterary affairs,[71] Podolyer's critique strikes—or, at least, aims—at the heart of imaginative literature. Not that one need worry about Podolyer's own deleterious effects on the common reader: he had already discredited himself quite thoroughly.

It is possible to view "Vi eltern darfn handlen" as both a coda and an ars poetica. Singer—whose own "Verter oder bilder" [Words or Pictures], we remember, expressed no less strong reservations about nonrealistic prose fiction—here defends, for the first time, the imaginative works he had been writing for over twenty years. Characteristically, Singer makes his argument not in one of Varshavski's earnest literary essays, but by playful implication: Podolyer disapproves of imaginative literature, and is a fool; hence writers who are not fools will have no such reservations.[72] If the syllogism is faulty, we may nonetheless be content that it provided Singer with theoretical sanction for his first overtly fantastic short stories since "Oyfn oylem-hatoye" [In the World of Chaos]:

Singer had already begun to publish extracts from "Dos gedenkbukh fun yeytser-hore" [The Devil's Memoirs] under his transparent pseudonym, Yitskhok Bashevis.[73] This decidedly nonrealistic series, as well as several later series of short stories with recurrent narrative situations, will be considered briefly in the following chapter.

Chapter 3

Fiction as Reportage, II: Recurrent Narrative Situations in the Later Works

I

Singer continued to write under the pseudonym D. Segal at least until the early 1960's,[1] and under the pseudonym Yitskhok Varshavski until he received the Nobel Prize in 1978. By the late 1940's, however, Singer had fairly well exhausted the innovative possibilities of these pseudonymous personas. Segal's pieces became increasingly pedestrian; many – anticipating the Ann Landers scandal by thirty years – were, in effect, rewrites of earlier columns.[2] Moreover, Segal discontinued, except for brief and rather uninteresting revivals through the latter 1950's, both his "Gast in der redaktsye" [Visitor to the Editorial Offices] series and his invitations to the readership to reply to troubling questions ostensibly occasioned by visitors or correspondents. Though all but twenty of Singer's periodical appearances in 1957 were signed D. Segal, for example, fully 47 of Segal's 120 pieces were titled "Vegn farsheydene zakhn" [Miscellania], a possible indication of the author's lack of interest in his bread-and-butter journalism;[3] a piece which promised the inauguration of a reader-response series –"Lezer shraybn" [Readers Write] – was abruptly halted after a single column.[4] For his part, Yitskhok Varshavski confined his limited output to book reviews and general literary essays. By the late 1950's, Singer was devoting the greater part of his attention to the creation of fictions – novels and short stories – signed Yitskhok Bashevis.

Bashevis' return to print was a gradual one – and one which cannot here be followed in its twistings and turnings, fits and starts. What is important to note is that Bashevis reemerged as the customary signature of Singer's fictions during the mid- and late 1940's.[5] This process was cautious: only eleven short stories saw print between 1943 and the end of the decade. Though a slim majority of these were discrete narratives told in the third person – among them several of Singer's better-known stories, including "Der spinozist: Dertseylung" [The Spinozan: A Story],[6] "Der kurtser fraytik" [Short Friday],[7] "Gimpl tam" [Gimpl the Fool],[8] and "Di kleyne shusterlekh" [The Little Shoemakers][9] – most were part of a projected series with demonic narrators; these often bore the subtitle "Fun der serye dertseylungen 'Dos gedenkbukh fun yeytser-hore' " [From the Series of Stories "The Devil's Diary"].[10] This series marked a number of departures for Singer, including the introduction of extended first-person narrative,[11] and, most importantly, a turn toward texts of unabashedly fantastic cast. A significant portion of Singer's oeuvre would henceforth be unambiguously fictional and hence beyond the scope of this study.

One might expect that Singer, having successfully overcome his early reservations about committing fiction, would cease to find it interesting or useful to shade these fictions back toward reportage. But, in fact, Singer was to exploit a number of recurring narrative situations toward precisely this end.

The most important of these was introduced in one of Bashevis' earliest reappearances – in the Rosheshone 1945 number of the *Yidisher kemfer*, political and cultural organ of the Labor Zionist Party (Farband) in New York City. Titled "Der katlen: A bobe-mayse" [The Wife Killer: An Old Wives' Tale],[12] it is narrated by an unnamed but certainly not uncharacterized old woman. We learn, for example, that she is from the real-world town of Turbin (as opposed to the purely fictional towns of the majority of Singer's contemporary fictions.[13] Moreover, we learn about both her narrative and social situation from her opening words:

Kegn dem vos ir zogt a katlonis? Bahit un bashirmt zol men vern, nisht do gedakht, nisht kegn nakht gedakht, s'zol oysgeyn tsu sonims kep un tsu zeyer laybn un lebn. Ikh shtam fun Turbin un dort iz geven a yid a katlen.

[As long as we're on the topic of wife-killing—may we be spared and protected, it shouldn't be thought of here, it shouldn't be thought of toward nightfall, it should fall on our enemies' heads and into their bodies and souls. I come from Turbin and there lived a Jew, a wife killer.] (p. 57)

The narrator is, by virtue of her malo-fugitive turns of speech,[14] a woman of a certain age and of the lower social classes. Further, the *ets-enk* second-person plural conjugation, once standard for all speakers of Central Yiddish, was, by the turn of the century, used only by the unlettered—especially by women.[15] Finally, we learn, both by the narrator's use of the second-person plural to her audience and by the opening sentence, that her story is occasioned by a remark, perhaps by an antecedent story, on the subject of wife-killing; that is, the story is a verbal reply to a verbal cue. The importance of developing a character in sufficient detail that the reader will recognize her reappearance—even after a considerable hiatus—will become apparent as the series develops and Singer attempts to ground this initially fictional character in the events of his own life.

One of the details which characterizes this narrator is her presention of herself as chronicler of actual events, rather than as a self-conscious shaper of fictions. As such, she is always anxious that her stories appear credible to her fictional auditors and, by implication, the reader. So, although the reader is prepared for a fantastic story by the subtitle "bobe-mayse" [old wives' tale], and although the narrator, by virtue of her cultural situation, might be expected to accept fantastic occurences as history, she does, in fact, tell a story which can be understood in naturalistic terms. That a man might, by dint of continuous unpleasantness, drive his wives to early graves is, after all, a proposition explicitly entertained by the narrator. It is only when his fourth and least likely wife persuades Pelte to transfer his entire wealth to her despite their open animosity that the narrator has recourse

to the townspeople's theory; she considers the possiblility that
Zlate had obtained a charm from the local sorcerer. The narrator,
for her part, casts considerable doubt upon the veracity of the
action she reports.

> Vos zi hot geton, fregt ets? Kh'veys nisht. Geredt hot men farshidn,
> nor male vos mentshn motlen. . . . Teyl hobn gezogt, az z'it im
> arayngeton a kishef in a knup, andere hobn ayngeroymt, az z'it
> farflokhtn a koltn.
> [What did she do, you ask? I don't know. People said various things,
> but there's no end to people's gossip. . . . Some said that she cast
> a spell on a knot; others whispered that she braided an elflock.]
> (p. 68)

Zlate's decision to seek a divorce from her impoverished husband,
even at the cost of a substantial settlement, and her death
moments before the divorce ceremony can be completed, are,
similarly, both over and undermotivated; the narrator, her fictive auditors, and the reader do not possess enough information
to mediate between psychological and supernatural explanations
of the decidedly odd goings-on. Rather than treat these events
as grist for a moral about the divine presence in the world – the
typical strategy of the bobe-mayse[16] – the narrator maintains her
stance as simple chronicler of events; she distances herself from
the most fabbling occurrences by reporting her own absence from
the scene –"Nor ikh bin demolt in Turbin nisht geven" [But I wasn't
in Turbin then] (pp. 73-74). This pose as historian will be main-
tained as her stories become increasingly fantastic.

There was no indication that the narrative situation of "Der
katlen" would be repeated, and, indeed, it was not for over a
decade. Moreover, even the series of first-person "Devil's Memoirs"
was soon abandoned. This does not mean that Singer stopped
writing overt fictions under the Bashevis pseudonym. Quite the
contrary: the ensuing twelve years saw the publication of Singer's
first novels since Der zindiker meshiekh [The Sinning Messiah] –
some four novels of varying length and kind in the course of
twelve years – as well as a considerable number of discrete short
stories signed Bashevis. Increasingly, though, the first-person narratives with which Singer reintroduced Bashevis did not reap-
pear until 1956, when Singer returned to his demonic narrators

in "Der shpigl: A monolog fun a shed" [The Mirror: A Monologue by a Demon][17] Though "Der shpigl" is narrated by a *shed* and the earlier series by a *yeytser-hore*, the narrative voice is, in fact, identical; the primary difference between the stories is that "Der shpigl" was an earlier story readied for publication some years after its writing; this would not be unique or even very unusual, considering Singer's working and publishing methods. but, in fact, the period of 1956-59 was to mark an unmistakable return to narrative situations eclipsed for nearly a decade.

The earliest first-person story with a human narrator from this period of reinvention is "Dos fayer" [The Fire],[18] told by one Leybush, a man on his deathbed in an unnamed poorhouse near Lublin. His use of the *ets-enk* conjugation, as well as his address to present but undescribed auditors, recalls the old woman narrator of "Der katlen":

> Yidn, kh'vil aykh dertseyln a mayse. S'iz nisht epes ka' mayse fun mayse-bikhl. S'iz geshen mit mir aleyn. Kh'hob ale yorn di zakh gehaltn besod, ober kh'lig shoyn in hekdesh un kh'vel fun dem dozikn bintl shtroy mer nisht oyfshteyn. Kh'shpir es, brider. Fun danen vet men mikh shoyn aroystrogn oyfn taare-bret. Vil ikh, ets zolt visn dem emes. [Jews, I'd like to tell you a story. It's not some kind of chapbook tale. It happened to me myself. I've kept it secret all these years, but I'm already lying here in the poorhouse and I won't be getting up from this bundle of straw again. I've got a feeling, brothers. From here they'll carry me to the morgue. So I'd like you to know the truth.] (p. 48)

Like the woman narrator, Leybush tells a tale the greater portion of which is best understood in psychological, rather than supernatural, terms: his father consistently favored Leybush's boorish but handsome brother, despite the brother's brazen neglect of his father and Leybush's years-long self-sacrifice on his father's behalf. Disinherited by his father and discredited as an arsonist by both his brother and the townspeople of his native Janow, Leybush decides to set his brother's house and mill afire. En route he finds them both already ablaze; at the risk of his own life and with foreknowledge that he would be blamed for having set the fire, Leybush rescues his brother and family whom he had intended to kill. As with Elke's appearance in a dream in "Gimpl tam" [Gimpl the Fool] – or the unlikely death of Peshe on the eve of her divorce – this story need not invoke supernatural explanations to account for its its occurrences; as in the earlier works, however, the supernatural explanation ("fun mayn kas hot zikh ongekhapt baym bruder s'hoyz" [my anger set fire to my brother's house]; p. 56) is as plausible – indeed, somewhat more plausible – than the naturalistic one. Here, in fact, no alternative explanation is offered though, of course, this does not preclude a more mundane origin of the fire.

As in "Der katlen," "Dos fayer" continues for some time – a relatively small amount of *Erzaehlzeit* but decades of *erzhaelte Zeit*! – before drawing to a close. Unlike the woman's narrative – which was embedded in a story-telling session, had not happened to the narrator herself, and, most importantly, did not depend on its veracity for its effect – Leybush's assertions of veracity both begin and conclude the narrative: "Itst, az kh'halt baym shtarbn, iz mayn viln m'zol visn dem emes. . . . [Now that I'm dying, it's my wish that the truth be known. . . .] (p. 56). The particular interest in "Dos fayer," and the reason I have willingly strayed from a discussion of Singer's female narrators to consider it, lies not only in its bibliographical position as first first-person narrative in nearly a decade, but, especially, in that it raises explicitly what was only implicit in "Der katlen"– namely, the acceptability of the embedded narrative as history. In so doing it is reminiscent of the project employed by Singer's pseudonymous personas Varshavski and Segal. A general concern with the border between fiction and reportage has been displaced from these putative authors to the narrator of this story. I shall return to this point in greater detail after considering two stories roughly contemporaneous with "Dos fayer"; both are narrated by old women very similar indeed to that of "Der katlen."

The first of these is "Der tsurikgeshrigener" [The Man Who Was Called Back].[19] Though this narrative appeared, uncharacteristically for Singer, without generic subtitle, the attentive reader might well recognize the return of the narrator of "Der katlen": her verbal tics, use of the *ets-enk* conjugation, and, especially, town of birth identify her as the same unnamed narrator:

Ets gleybt nisht, kinderlekh? S'zenen do tsurigeshrigene. Eynem hob ikh aleyn gekent vayl r'hot gevoynt bay undz in shtot. Ets vilt hern? Vel ikh enk dertseyln. S'iz geven bay undz in Turbin a yid a nogid. Nisht far aykh gedakht, nisht far keynem gedakht, iz er gevorn mesukn-shlaf. [You don't believe me, children? There *are* people who have been called back. I knew one myself since he lived in our town. You want to hear more? I'll tell you. A wealthy Jew lived in our town of Turbin. It shouldn't happen to you, it shouldn't happen to anyone, but he fell deathly ill. (p. 51)

There is little need for extensive consideration of "Der tsurikgeshrigener," for it follows both in plot and narrative situation the pattern set by "Der katlen." Again, the narrator is an old woman of lower social status; her story admits of a (less persuasive) quotidien explanation and of a (more persuasive) supernatural one; narration continues well past the point of resolution; a variety of distancing devices are employed to protect the narrator from asserting the veracity of the non-naturalistic occurrences. The reader is not surprised when, for example, he or she is told that a wife's deafening exhortations to her presumably dying husband are eventually followed by his revival and recovery, albeit with greatly changed personality: the reported events per se do not require a suspension of disbelief beyond that of accepting the narrative frame itself.

The narrator maintains this stance to the end, even in her second-hand report of events barely, if at all, amenable to naturalistic interpretation:

Ikh hob im toyterheyt nisht gezen, kh'bin demolt geven a vaybl in di hoykhe khadoshim. Nor di vos zenen gegangen im onkukn hobn geshvoyrn, az r'hot oysgezen vi a mes vos m'hot oysgegrobn fun keyver. . . . Bay der taale zol zikh hobn opgebrokhn a hant mit a fus. Kh'bin demolt nisht geven derbay, nor far vos zoln mentshn oystrakhtn? [I didn't see him dead; I was pregnant and nearly ready to give birth. But those who went to see him swore that he looked like a corpse that someone had dug up from the grave. . . . At his laying-out a hand and a foot were said to have broken off. I wasn't there, but why should people make things up?] (p. 61)

In her efforts to distance herself from the story's only overtly supernatural event – Alter's nearly instantaneous decomposition after his second death – the narrator vouches only for the accuracy with which she has chronicled others' observations, not for the veracity of those observations themselves. Indeed, she places herself at some spatial remove from these concluding goings-on, which are more coda than conclusion: her own role in the story had ended with Alter's death. Finally, she makes use of the formal and uncommon (especially in spoken Yiddish) syntactical form for recording reported events in the past for which one does not personally vouch — *zol zikh hobn* + participle, rather than the somewhat formal *men* + compound past or the colloquial *mentshn* + compound past. In so doing, the narrator preserves her position as neutral chronicler of occurrences to which she was eyewitness, also preserving thereby the status of her verbal artifacts as historical reportage.

At the same time, however, we sense in this story the narrator's own pull toward the very fantastic interpretations from which she has taken such pains to protect her narrative. For one thing, she sees no reason to mistrust the townspeople ("Why should people make things up?"), failing to see therein the collective production of popular fiction. Though the formal cast of her narrative remains strictly reportorial, her interpretive asides owe more to the genre of *bobe-mayse*[20] than to that of chronicle.

We have, not uncharacteristically, a narrative embedded in a fictional frame. that narrative itself is generically ambiguous: formally, it derives its authority from its claims to historical reportage — the eyewitness narrator's eschewal of all non-quotidien narrative elements, her penchant for both relevant and nonrelevant detail underscore the text's function as chronicle; thematically, however, it derives its interest from the questions of supernatural intervention it raises — and these, in turn, are predicated upon a reading of events as *bobe-mayse*. Singer's narrator has here done what Singer had earlier done in the guise of his pseudonymous journalistic personas — namely, blurred the distinction between reportage and fiction.

It remained for Singer to address himself to the frame of these stories. To this point, they appeard to be of unambiguous fictionality. Matters were not long to remain this unproblematic.

II

During these ten years, Singer continued to write longer works of varying genre and literary quality; these include *Di familye Mushkat* [The Family Mushkat] (1945-48), *Der feter fun Amerike* [The Uncle from America] (1949-51), *Shotns baym Hodson* [*Shadows by the Hudson*] (1957), *A shif keyn Amerike* [A Ship to America] (1958), *Der kuntsnmakher fun Lublin* [The Magician of Lublin] (1959), and *Der knekht* [The Slave] (1961). The most interesting of Singer's longer works, however, were a series of memoirs signed Yitskohk Varshavski. Although the titles of these memoirs differed – they include *Mayn tatns bezdn-shtub* [My Father's Rabbinical Court, translated as *In My Father's Court*] (1955)[21] and *Der shrayberklub* [The Writers' Club] (1956)[22] – each consisted of a series of some fifty to one hundred pieces of from 1000 to 1500 words each, generally published twice weekly in the *Forverts* (*Jewish Daily Forward*). They represent, I would argue, Singer's most significant publications of the 1950's; to the Yiddish readership, at least, these remain Singer's central book-length texts.[23]

A common element of these memoirs is that all the segments are narrated in the first person by the putative author, Yitskhok Varshavsk. the sole exception, to the best of my knowledge, among these nearly 1000 episodes is one entitled "Di mume Yentl" [Aunt Yentl], a monologue in the unmediated voice of the title character.[24]

One gets only the briefest glimpses of Mume Yentl before she begins her chapter-long narrative. When she is first introduced, Yentl is simply part of the scenery – the wife of Varshavski's Feter Yoysef, a hassidic rabbi and his mother's brother. Her physical description – unimportant in the context of this memoir – will later help the reader identify her as the old woman narrator of the previous fictions:

Nokhn feter Yoysef is gegangen mit vakldikn gang a breyte yidene, di mume Yentl, dem feter Yoysefs drit vayb. . . . Azoy vi der feter Yoysef iz geven shmol un flink, azoy iz di dozike yidene . . . geven breyt, shver, gelasik. [Walking after Feter Yoysef with a wavering fait was an amply-built Jewish woman, Mume Yentl, Feter Yoysef's third wife. . . . Just as Feter Yoysef was thin and agile, she was broad, heavy, sedentary.][25]

Though she is undoubtedly an interesting character, there is no indication, at this point, of the unique position she is to occupy in *Mayn tatns bezdn-shtub.*

Her tale itself is unremarkable. Mume Yentl recalls her first marriage – happy save for her childlessness, her second marriage – financially comfortable but loveless, her third marriage – about which she is diplomatically silent. Varshavski claims to have included the chapter only as example of Mume Yentl's verbal craft; his remark upon its conclusion is "Ot azoy hot geredt mayn mume Yentl. Ikh hob gekent zitsn shoen un zikh tsuhern tsu ire reyd un mayses" [This is the way my Aunt Yentl spoke. I could have sat for hours listening to her talk and stories] (p. 331).

Yentl's narrative stands in sharp contrast to nearly each of the chapters which made its way through Singer's two successive cullings – first, of the hundred-odd pieces which appeared in the *Forverts* to the sixty collected in the Yiddish edition of *Mayn tatns bezdn-shtub*, and second, of these sixty to the forty-nine included in *In My Father's Court* when it appeared eleven years later.[26]

If the substance of Mume Yentl's monologue does not reward close scrutiny, her verbal performance certainly does. It reproduces her central Yiddish dialect and somewhat archaic idiolect (e.g. the use of the *ets-enk* conjugation and of an uninflected adjective after a singular personal pronoun, both formerly common in Central Yiddish but rejected by Modern Standard Yiddish and all but absent from cultivated speech in the twentieth century). Most importantly, however, her speech gives the attentive Yiddish reader an historical referent for the unnamed narrators of the stories with female narrators: Mume Yentl's voice in *Mayn tatns bedznshtub* is identical to the narrative voice of the previously-discussed fictions.

Two rather uncommon turns of phrase – the first an apostrophe to her auditor(s), the second an archaic malo-fugitive expression – link Mume Yentl to the female narrators of Bashevis' previous fictions, as the following should make clear:

Mayn lib mentsh – hot di mume Yentl geredt tsu mayn muter ["My dear person," said Mume Yentl to my mother] ("Di mume Yentl," p. 331).
Mayne libe mentshn, ets redt vegn nokhmakhn? ["My dear people, you're talking about imitation?"] ("Getsl malpe," p. 165).
Mayne libe mentshn, r'iz antlofn fun ir ["My dear people, he ran away from her"] ("Hene fayer," p. 306).

* * * * *

[Pelte] hot gehat fir vayber un s'zol tsu keyn gnay nisht zayn – r'hot zey ale avekgeshikt [(Pelte) had four wives and, with all due respect, he sent them all to the other world] ("Der katlen," p. 57).
Ober di Motyekhe, s'zol tsu keyn gnay nisht zayn, hot im keseyder nor shtakhelirt [But Motye's wife, with all due respect, did nothing but tease him] ("Kleyn un groys," p. 248).

Lest there be any doubt about the narrator's identity, "Der katlen" and "Der tsurikgeshrigener" explicity locate their action in the shtetl of Turbin; Mume Yentl, we remember, lived with her second husband in Turbin. What, before the publication of *Mayn tatns bezdn-shtub*, might have been a private, hence pre-literary, borrowing by Singer from his own experience becomes, with its appearance in print, public play – a juxtaposition of one set of overt fictions with another set of nonfictional memoirs.

Singer complicates what is already a complex situation by casting doubt upon the strict historicity of his memoirs. To be sure, any attempt at "telling lives" requires shaping of experience, especially when, as with Singer, that experience is used as the basis for exploring moral questions.[27] Moreover, even the untutored reader might be expected to naturalize such insistently literary texts in the same ways in which he or she naturalizes other literary texts, notwithstanding concurrent textual clues which encourage one to treat the text as nonfictional memoir: short fictions are (or were, before the Holocaust) the dominant mode of Yiddish literary expression; by contrast, personal memoirs are (or were, before the Holocaust) a relatively infrequent form, the codes of which were, in the mid-1950's, still relatively unfamiliar to the common reader. But it is the "Author's Note" to *In My Father's Court* which forces the issue. In it, Singer (and not his memoiristic persona) writes that "*In My Father's Court*

. . . is in a certain sense a literary experiment. It is an attempt to combine two styles – that of memoirs and that of belles-lettres – and its approach to description and its manner of conveying situations differ from those used in my other writings."[28] It is important to remember that Yiddish has no common expression for *belles-lettres*; its cognate, *beletristik*, means in Yiddish – as it does in its Polish and Russian forms –"fiction." It seems clear that Singer is claiming for his book a status somewhere between fiction and reportage; since, moreover, this claim appears not in a postscript or discrete article, but as preface to the work itself, it may be taken not as much as critical observation as normative in struction to the reader. To read *Mayn tatns bezdn-shtub* correctly, then, one must be aware of its ontological instability.

This has, of course, implications for the apprehension and interpretation of the work as a whole. For the purpose at hand, however, it is important to see how "Di mume Yentl" both anchors Singer's more overtly fictional texts in a nonfictional historical setting and, simultaneously, calls into question the strict historicity of that setting. Just as the female narrators blur distinctions between fiction and reportage within the fictional frame, Singer blurs those distinctions in the frame itself. Once again, Singer has begun an experiment modestly enough and, over the course of time, tested its formal limits with ever more radical undermining of generic norms. This particular experiment, as we shall see, had yet to be concluded.

I

Neither Bashevis' recurrent female narrator nor Varshavski's Mume Yentl appeared for nearly a decade following the publication of *Mayn tatns bezdn-shtub*. One might well have assumed that this particular experiment in blurring the distinction between fiction and reportage had run its course, to be repaced by other experiments or, for that matter, other projects. But, in fact, the unnamed woman narrator returns in two short stories published in 1966, "Tsaytl un Rikl" [Tsaytl and Rikl] and "Di nodl" [The Needle].[29] These stories continue the pattern first established in "Der katlen" some twenty-one years earlier. The only difference lies in the exaggeration of those verbal tics and turns of phrase by which the reader identifies the narrator as the familiar old woman of the earlier stories. In "Di nodl," for example, a story of unexceptional length, the narration is once prefaced by "mayne gute mentshn" [my good people] (p. 101) and twice – within a page of one another – by "mayne libe mentshn" [my dear people] (pp. 107, 108). This piling-on of apostrophe to the unseen fictive auditors allows Singer's readers several opportunities to refresh their memories and renew the link between these new stories and those of similar cast which preceded them.

Whether any but the most astute reader would have recalled the connection between Bashevis' old woman narrator and Varshaviski's own Mume Yentl is a bit more questionable. To be sure, Singer had demanded even more acuity and recall of readers in the past. Here, though, one is expected to draw connections across boundaries which are at once chronological, generic, and authorial. Lest there be any doubt that the old woman of these narratives is indeed Varshavski's Mume Yentl, Singer subtitles "Bendit un Dishke" [Bendit and Dishke], a story written in about 1956,[30] "Der mume Yentls a monolog" [A Monologue by Mume Yentl]. Thus Yitskhok Bashevis, a putative author of fictions, chooses to make explicit for the first time that his stories are monologues spoken by the aunt of Yitskhok Varshavski, a putative author of memoirs. By this time, of course, there was little real doubt about the identity of Bashevis or Varshavski: *Mayn Tatns bezdn-shtub* had appeared in a Yiddish selective culling in 1956 under the signature Yitskhok Bashevis, and, in 1966, in English translation as *In My Father's Court* under the signature Isaac Bashevis Singer. But what is at stake here is the dicreteness of Singer's pseudonymous personas, and not the readers' knowledge of the historical author's identity: to this day, Singer's readership refers to his works by the name of their putative author (Varshavski, Segal, Bashevis), and nearly never by that of their real-world author (Zinger, or Bashevis-Zinger), which appears only on the spines of Singer's books in academic editions; on other volumes, as in articles and even encyclopedia entries,[31] Singer's pseudonymous personas lead separate lives. Singer, who has, for

the most part, ultimate say about the attribution of those pieces
first appearing in the *Forverts*, has worked hard to preserve these
distinctions.

I have, thus far, plotted my discussion in primarily
chronological terms, not only because this permits a degree of
ordering of Singer's writings but, more importantly, because
Singer tends to move from less to more radically experimental
texts within a particular narrative strategy. During the final decade
in which Mume Yentl was to appear – from approximately 1969
through approximately 1979 – Singer follows a different strategy,
and one a bit less amenable to chronological discussion:
previously-introduced narrative forms continue to appear (closed
monologues with or without ascription to Mume Yentl, open
monologues with a greater or lesser degree of opening of the narrative frame), and new narrative forms join the corpus, themselves
to repeat as yet newer forms are introduced.

At the same time the physical characterization of Yentl
remains consistent, although details are added which serve further to identify the historical and fictional Mume Yentl. In "Oyf
der potshine" [On the Sidewalk],[32] for example, we learn where,
when and for whom Yentl tells her tale:

> Shabes nokhn tsholnt zenen zey gezesn oyf der potshine un dert-
> seylt mayses: Blimele Fishls, Yentl di rebitsin un Gnendele. [After
> the Sabbath stew they sat (on benches) on the sidewalk and told
> stories – Fishl's wife Blimele, Yentl the rabbi's wife, and Gnendele]
> (p. 75).

Although Yentl receives only secondary billing in this trio of old
wives' tales, it becomes clear that hers is the primary storytelling role: she receives considerably more *Erzaehlzeit* than do her
friends and foils; she leads discussion of all three tales; and the
reader receives a considerably fuller description of her person
and attire:

> Yentl di rebitsin hot getrogn a kopke mit a hoykhn tshipik un mit
> altesene bender fun dray kolirn: grin, gel, bloy. Zi iz shoy geven
> dem rovs drite vayb. Freir iz zi gezesn an almone nokh a
> gutsbazitser. Zi hot gehat ongehkoyft in di raykhe yorn a sakh
> tsirung, un shabes hot zi dos ongeton. [Yentl the rabbi's wife wore

a decorative headdress high on her forehead with old-fashioned
ribbons in three colors – green, yellow, blue. She was the rabbi's
third wife. Before that she'd been a widow of a property owner.
She had bought a lot of jewelry in her wealthy years, which she
wore on the Sabbath.] (p. 75).

Her physical description will, as we shall see, act as an additional
device for identifying Yentl as an intertextual constant.

Mume Yentl enjoys nearly uninterrupted reign as central
character in the stories which followed; interruptions by her
auditors are typically silenced with a preemptory "Khaptts nisht
[Not so fast]. Yentl's centrality is, however, a good deal less absolute when she vies for the reader's attention not with her fictional
auditors, but, rather, with the youthful Varshavski:

Di mume Yentl hot gevorfn a blik oyf mir.
– Host lib mayses, ha?
– Yo, mume. Shtark.
– Vos kumt aroys fun mayses? Beser zog peyrek.
[Aunt Yentl glanced at me.
"You like stories, huh?"
"Yes, Aunt (Yentl). Very much."
"What's the use of stories? Better study Scripture."][33]

There is relatively little of Varshavski here. Unlike the chapter
of *Mayn tatns bezdn-shtub*, which, characteristically, end with
musings – either those of the youthful Varshavski or those of the
retrospective memoirist – on the import of the narrated events,
this narrator yields to Mume Yentl on matters of interpretation;
the inset story belongs, after all, to her. In later stories with this
frame, the first-person narrator is not as circumspect. "Not for
the Sabath," Singer's latest such story and one which, if I am not
mistaken, has yet to appear in the original Yiddish,[34] juxtaposes
Yentl's rather straightforward and non-introspective narrative with
the child's more associative and speculative reported thought: "I
sat on an oak mortar that was used to grind matzo meal. Through
the cracks the sun reflected the colors of the rainbow in the
floating dust" (p. 170). Withal, Yentl's is the primary storytelling impulse and the locus of the reader's attention. But Singer
has continued to open the narrative frame even wider to an

unmistakably Singer-like character-participant. I shall return to a concluding discussion of this narrator-participant after a brief examination of the embedded narratives themselves.

IV

The frames of Singer's Mume Yentl stories were, steadily if not always consistently, opening to admit ever more data on the narrative situation, as well as on the young Varshavski as character-auditor. The result, as we have seen, were stories of ever more memoiristic cast, at least as regards their frame setting. At the same time as the frame narratives were moving from the more to the less overlty fictitious, the embedded narratives were undergoing a counter-movement – from the more to the less reportorial. If "Der Katlen," for example, was best understood – despite the narrator's hedged urgings – in naturalistic, psychological terms, and if even the later narratives – both situationally and in response to the narrator's disclaimers – could have also been taken as oral chronicles, Mume Yentl's embedded stories of the early 1970's defy naturalization as strict reportage.

"Der lantukh" [The *Lantukh*], which appeared in 1970 under the signature Yitskhok Bashevis, is typical.[35] It is told to Varshavski's mother and, we find out somewhat into the frame narrative, to the young Varshavski as well; this is, one might note in passing, another step toward autobiographical memoir: the reader has had no contextual clues about the historicity of Mume Yentl's earlier auditors, named or unnamed, but Singer's mother is described at length in the memoirs and commemorated in the *Bashevis* pseudonym.[36]

In contrast to the memoiristic cast of the narrative frame, Yentl's story itself not ony presupposes, but actually hinges upon, the existence of *lantukher*, or domestic imps. It details the successive withdrawal from social intercourse of three women – a widowed mother who takes to bed at her husband's premature death and never leaves it; her daughter, divorced and abandoned; and her granddaughter, a happy youth who finally succumbs to her mother and grandmother's morbidity and, like them, never leaves the house. This much of the story is all too comprehensible in psychological terms, and the narrator does indeed attempt to make sense of her narrative in this way. But "Der lantukh" is no *Casa de Bernarda Alba*; the naturalistic narrative is first called into question for the most naturalistic of reasons: the three women manage to survive without any apparent source of income, and without leaving their home even to shop for necessities.

There are the customary hedgings of the I-wasn't-there variety. We are told, for example, that "farlofn iz es take in Turbin un ongehoybn hot zih es yorn eyder mir zenen gekumen ahin" [This all took place in Turbin and had begun years before we arrived there] (p. 45). In her zeal for detail and anecdote, Mume Yentl also relates whisps of information which, had to three women been more inclined to explain themselves to the community, might have provided explanations for at least some of the causes of communal consternation. While chronicling the family's secretiveness, for example, Mume Yentl recounts how "der potsht- treger hot a mol gebrakht der mishpokhe a briv farziglt mit trivaks – fun vanen veyst men nisht" [the postman once brought the family a letter sealed with sealing wax – one didn't know from where] (p. 49); this letter might well account for the family's eco- nomic situation, especially since the daughter's ex-husband had departed for the big city. Moreover, the granddaughter did, in fact, go shopping – perhaps more frequently than the narrator chooses to remember: "Fun mol tsu mol hot zi epes gekoyft in a gevelbl" [From time to time she bought something in a shop] (p. 49). Also, the townspeople based their earliest – and many of their subsequent – convictions that the family shared their house with a *lantukh* on the word of nighttime passers-by, or simply on their imaginations: the night watchman, for example, reported that the granddaughter often laughed at night – proof positive that she was being tickled by the *lantukh* (p. 50) and the fact that the family was provided with wood and water was, ipso facto, taken as evidence that the *lantukh* had been their provider (p. 47). Finally, the very ardor and obious partisanship of the narrator (her first sentence, and the first sentence of "Der lantukh," was "S'zenen do lantukher" [There *are lantukher*; p. 44), might encour- age the reader to dismiss both Mume Yentl's version of the events she chronicles and the community's even less cautious construal of these events.

The reader is thus likely to discount the supernatural accretions on what is, in the main, a narrative not in need of such accretions in making sense of the reported events; this is especially true in the context of the readers' previous experience with Mume Yentl's (and the unnamed female narrator's) rather straightforward, if sensational chronicles. Yet there are supernatural elements in "Der lantukh" which are not as easily brushed away. Consider, for example, the account of Motl Bentses, who was sent to check on the well-being of the women after a snowfall:

> Er kumt tsu un dos gantse gebey is farzunken in shney. . . . Nor er hot great a lopete un genumen grobn. . . . Azoy vi er grobt hert er fun yener zayt a skripen un a geshnorkh: m'grobt dort oykh. . . . S'efnt zikh a veg un er derzet a pitsele mentshele, breyter vi lenger. . . . Motl Bentses heybt on tsu redn tsu im un yener tut a shtek aroys a tsung fun moyl biz tsum nopl. . . . Dos iz geven der lantukh. [When he got there the whole house was buried in snow. . . . But he had a shovel and began to dig. . . . While he was digging he heard grating and scratching from the other side: they're digging there, too. . . . A path opened and he saw a tiny man, broader than he was tall. . . . Motl Bentses had begun to speak to him when he stuck out his tongue all the way to his navel. That was the *lantukh.*] (pp. 47-48)

Yentl, to be sure, is persuaded of the existence of the *lantukh,* and hardly brings a critical eye to Motl Bentses' story. In fact, she introduces it by insisting: "Kh'hob frier gezogt az m'kon zey nisht zen. M'hot im gezen!" [I said before that they can't be seen. He *was* seen!] (p. 47). we are told – a bit of residual hedging? – that the sighting of the *lantukh* took place at dusk. Nonetheless, Motl Bentses certainly had no doubt about what he saw nor, if the narrator is to be believed at all, was he predisposed to encounter the supernatural; the fact that he sought out the rabbi, who, in turn, saw that the account was recorded in the *pinkes* – an official record of the major events in a community's history – showed the earnestness, at least, of Motl Bentses' claim.

Finally, the story concludes with another eye-witness account, that of the Turbin fire marshall who describes how a bizarre creature, "a tsure-meshune, nisht ka' mentsh un nisht ka' khaye, nor a bashefenish, halb-hunt, halb-malpe, mit tsoytn un kaltenes" [strange-faced, neither man nor beast, but rather a creature – half-dog and half-monkey – with shaggy hair and elflocks] (p. 50), came to his door one night to report the fire which was to kill the three women – and only these three – in their home.

So, for the first time in these narratives, it is nearly impossible to make sense of the events without accepting the possibility of supernatural interventionl. This necessity severely undermines Mume Yentl's presentation of herself as a simple memoirist. Although the reader is encouraged to see "Der lantukh" as yet another in the series of Mume Yentl's chronicles – through expectations from her earlier narratives, the presumed historicity of the narrative frame, the psychological coherence of the women's behavior and the narrator's hedgings – the story, by virtue of its fantastic elements, cannot be seen as anything other than fiction. This is yet another example of Singer's progression from less to more experimental texts, and from those which accept to those which challenge generic distinctions. As the narrative frames of the pieces with old women narrators have shaded from fiction to reportage, the embedded narratives themselves have shaded from near-naturalistic to overtly supernatural – a process which confirms their fictiveness. this development is carried forward in another of Singer's stories, also entitled "The Lantuch."

This latter story is one of Singer's growing numbers of pieces for children, which, as a rule, appear only in English translation.[36] The first surprise is, and should be, the work's title. Singer does not casually recycle titles; indeed, he frequently alludes to titles of his works after lapses of many years, across genres, and with a playfulness which demands recognition by the reader of allusions not otherwise signalled. with this in mind, there is little doubt that, from the start, the latter version of "The Lantuch" is meant to stand in juxtaposition with the earlier, even if the child reader or auditor is presumably innocent of such knowledge. And, in fact, the briefest glimpse at this story confirms its connectedness to the pieces for adults.

As befits a children's story, "The Lantuch" is rather short – barely six pages of large type, as contrasted to the ten pages of considerably smaller type of the earlier version. Nonetheless, its narrative frame is not only considerably longer than that of "Der lantukh"; it is also considerably longer than Mume Yentl's embedded narrative itself – in sharp contrast to the conventions of the adult series. And the young Singer, who had figured only marginally even in the pieces with first-person frames, is here the central character; moreover, the older Singer, who narrates this story in the first person, has, by virtue of his status as memoirist, omniscient access to a single consciousness – his own. Thus we are doubly encouraged to consider assertions made in the narrative voice as normative and historically reliable. Lastly, the gently didactic tone of the children's story invites the reader to "belive him- or herself into" (as one says in Yiddish) the non-critical role of child reader or auditor.

Mume Yentl, who, uniquely, belongs to both the narrative frame and the embedded story, would appear, at least initially, to be the same historical mediating intellect as in the piece's adult namesake; she tells her story in the same attire, and on the same occasion, as in "Der lantukh": "For the Sabbath, my aunt wore a dress sown with arabesques and a bonnet with glass beads, festooned with green, red, and blue ribbons" (p. 52). She also has the same verbal tics, though one does have to wait several pages for the familiar "My dear people" apostrophe (p. 56). Finally, the stories have many plot elements in common. Three factors combine, then, to persuade the reader that he or she is reading the typical Mume Yental story, albeit written for a younger audience: expectations engendered by the series of stories with old women narrators as a whole, expectations engendered by a title shared with an earlier, similar story; and expectations reinforced by concrete similarities between both stories. thus it is all the more surprising that Singer should have singled out "The Lantuch" for a number of rather substantial revisions of a pattern then nearly thirty years in the making.

The first indication the reader has that something is different is the straightforwardness both in substance and report of the two supernatural sightings. In contrast to the *erlebte Rede* of the reports in "Der lantukh,"[37] both sightings are recounted here by Yentl in the voice of an omniscient narrator, who even adds glosses to the reported actions. In the first case, a village youth walks by the homebound women's house at night:

He opened the gate to the courtyard and saw an ax swinging and chips flying, but there was no one there. It was the lantuch chop-

ping wood for the winter. The next day, when the youth revealed
what he had seen, people laughed at him. . . . But it was true.
(p. 56)

Not merely the youth, but the narrator as well, stake their reputations for veracity on the literal historicity of their observations.
Mume Yentl is even more emphatic in her defense of the ship-
ping agent who sees two pails being lowered into a well and
carried, as if by one invisible, to the house where the women
lived: "This Meir David was an honest man and not one to make
up things" (p. 57). To disbelieve the witness is to disbelieve both
the tale and its teller.

There were, we remember, details rather casually introduced
in the earlier story which might, given a bit more corroborative
detail, have mooted the entire mystery of the familial income and
how the shopping got done. As it was, the reader was offered
at least the fragments of a naturalistic interpretation of events.
Here, however, that possibility is definitely foreclosed: there is
no absent former spouse in this story, and no one ever left home
to shop for provisions. Most importantly, however, the characters
and their situations have been rearranged so that the reader
wishes a beneficient *lantukh* to have been present, regardless of
his or her predisposition toward the supernatural.

For one thing, the characters – here two women, an ill and
widowed mother and her blind, invalid daughter – do not will
themselves into seclusion; theyu are confined to their home of
necessity. For another, both are attractive and innocent. Sum-
moned to the rabbi to explain the strange goings-on, the daughter
answers frankly: " 'Someone provides for us, but who it is I do
not know. It must be an angel from heaven' " (p. 57). It would
seem uncharitable to begrudge these unfortunates help from
whatever source, or to delve too deeply into their private lives.

Also atypically, Mume Yentl was present in town from the
story's beginning through to its conclusion many years later;
though never an eye witness, she does not allow (or, as in previous
stories, invite) her auditors to make allowances for a possible
errors or omissions in her chronicle. Finally, the narrator's tone
of straightforward acceptance of the stuff of her narrative, coupled
with a similarly straightforward assumption that her tale will also
be perceived by her auditors as interesting but unproblematic,

does not encourage the more critical mindset brought to her other chronicles. Even the nearly identical first sentences of "Der lan- tukh" and "The Lantuch" work quite differently in context. The former asserts the existence of *lantukher*, whishing, however, that the assertion were false; presumably, the narrator would be quite content to have the basis of her story pulled out from under her. Moreover, the very emphaticness of her initial assertion antici- pates scepticism on the part of her auditors: "S'zenen do lantukher, hot mayn mume Yentl gezogt. Halevay volt nisht geven" ["There *are lantukher*," said my Aunt Yentl. "Would that there weren't"] (p. 44). Compare this to the beginning of Yentl's narrative proper in "The Lantuch":

> A lantuch? Yes, there is such a spirit as a lantuch. These days people don't believe in such things, but in my time they knew that everything can't be explained away with reason. The world is full of secrets. (p. 53)

Mume Yentl does not anticipate resistance to her statement, nor does she wish that it were false. She is for the attentive reader, supported by Singer as implied author, because the last two sentences, while atypical for Mume Yentl, are recurring formulae in Varshavski's memoirs and, later, in Bashevis' stories with Singer- like narrators.[38] Furthermore, she does not consider the matter unfit for childish ears and imaginations. In contrast to the Yentl who shoos her nephew away and admonishes him to read Scrip- ture, this Yentl speaks in a language sufficiently simple for a child to understand; though the child's mother, as well as two visiting older female neighbors, are present for Mume Yentl's verbal performance, the young man is clearly her intended auditor, the adult females the societally-mandated audience for this type of speech act.

"The Lantuch" was published in a collection of stories of chil- dren. This would appear to moot the question of suspension of disbelief, for in what other genre is the reader expected to accept the existence of supernatural beings with such equanimity?[39]

And, I would suggest, the existence of the titular *lantukh* is indeed granted an extra measure of credence by the story's generic identification as a work for younger audiences. But it is also important to note that the collection in which it appears, *Naftali the Storyteller and His Horse, Sus, and Other Stories*, contains not a single other overtly fantastic text.

Indeed, two stories in the collection –"A Hanukkah Eve in Warsaw," which directly follows "The Lantuch," and "Growing Up," the collection's concluding piece – make direct claim to literal historicity: both are autobiographical first-person sketches containing much in the way of externally-corroberable data. The first mentions Singer's family by name and their residence by address: "We – my parents, my older brother Joshua, my sister Hindele, my younger brother Moshe, and I – lived at 10 Krochmalna Street. . . ." (p. 63). In the latter, he announces his plans to write a book titled *Into the Wild Forest*; though they do not come to fruition within the frame of "Growing Up," Singer did, in fact, author a children's fiction titled *Alone in the Wild Forest*.[40] These memoiristic pieces claim a literal historicity of the most explicit sort, further embedding Mume Yentl's narrative in a nonfictional matrix. Thus Mume Yentl's story of the *lantukh* is twice framed – by the frame narrative proper and by the stories preceding and following it in the collection. Both frames are historical and reportorial, suggesting that the embedded story might also best be naturalized as reportage. Of course, I do not suggest that the reader – adult or child – will entirely succeed in so doing, or that success in taking the story of the *lantukh* as reportage is any more of a literary than it is a pedagogical desideratum. What I do suggest is that this is yet another case of Singer blurring the distinctions between fiction and reportage, and, within the series of stories with old woman narrators, the most radically experimental thus far. That he had done this in the context of an otherwise innocent children's story is all the more remarkable.

V

Singer continued to write Mume Yentl stories at least through 1979, though their frequency and, arguably, also their quality, began to trail off markedly by the end of the decade. Though it would be imprudent to predict their disappearance from the oeuvre – we remember that decades-long interval between "Der katlen" and the introduction of Mume Yentl as named narrator – they have not figured largely in Singer's most recent production. The most noteworthy recurrent narrative situation in the recent oeuvre has, however, been one which also juxtaposes historical and autobiographical elements against what are frequently unusual and possibly supernatural events. These are the stories featuring, and almost invariably narrated in the first person by, an aging Yiddish writer who resembles ever more the actual Isaac Bashevis Singer. In the course of several dozen such narratives, we learn that he lives in Manhattan; had once lived in Brooklyn and, earlier yet, in Poland;[41] writes for a daily Yiddish newspaper, often on non-fictional topics;[42] is besieged by admirers, who are cordially received but pressed for their life stories;[43] goes on frequent lecture tours;[44] is forgetful and bewildered by strange surroundings,[45] etc. On the other hand, there are infrequent but persistent reminders that this central character is not to be identified with the historical Isaac Singer *tout court*: publicly-known facts about Singer's person and oeuvre are violated – in one early story, for example, this character is named Kohen[46] – but not in the consistent manner which would create of this Singer-like character a persona different from its historical analogue. In fact, no such alternate character is permitted to emerge; one is left with the historical Singer as the only consistent persona, but modified on an *ad hoc* basis sufficiently to dissuade all but the most naive of readers from treating the stories as nonproblematic memoiristic reportage.

It would be both difficult and unprofitable to explore this Singer-like character in particular detail, since few of the stories in which he appears have, apparently, seen print in their original Yiddish versions; not one has been collected in the Yiddish editions of Singer's works, though a short novel, *Der bal-tshuve* [The Penitent], which features this narrative situation was published in Tel Aviv in 1971 and in English translation some twelve years later.[47] It is possible that a more detailed bibliographical knowledge of Singer's recent oeuvre – now entirely lacking – would permit the location of at least some of these fictions but, for the time being, they are available only in translation and without any reliable indication of the sequence of their authorship or publication. In light of these considerations, a systematic survey of these stories is best deferred.

There is, however, one story in this series which should be considered in any discussion of Mume Yentl, a story which purports to follow the career of one of her descendents. It was, one can argue with the benefit of hindsight, all but inevitable that Singer's two most consistently-developed recurrent narrative lines should someday intersect. And, in fact, they do in a short story titled "Hanka,"[48] a rather detailed consideration of which will end this chapter.

"Hanka," not uniquely among the stories with Singer-like narrators, purports to recount the events on a lecture tour – here, an extended journey by ship to Buenos Aires and thence to the Argentine hinterlands. Unlike the Mume Yentl stories, which were several times mediated (Yentl repeating someone's report of a set of events, filtered through a young boy's consciousness, and, finally, through that of the putative author – that same young boy grown up), "Hanka" 's narrator himself vouches for the literal historicity of the events narrated; he is both central character and narrator and, as we are led to suspect, much like – though not identical to – the historical Isaac Singer.

Initial historical allusions are to extraliterary, independently-known facts of Singer's life, i.e. that he is a Yiddish writer of a certain age residing in New York; that he undertakes lecture tours. Unlike the other stories with Singer-like narrators with which I am familiar, however, the first extended link between this work and prior knowledge brought to it by the intended readership is not as much through biographical data as through previously-encountered quasi-biographical texts, i.e. the Mume Yentl narratives. Waiting for the narrator at the dockside are his impresario and a young woman –

> a yunge froy vos hot zikh foregshtelt vi mayne a kroyve. Geheysn hot zi Hanka un geven iz zi, vi zi hot gezogt, an eynikl fun mayn mume Yentl mit ir ershtn man. Hanka iz faktish nisht geven mayn kroyve vayl mayn feter Arn iz geven Yentls a driter man [a young woman who introduced herself as a relative of mine. Her name was Hanka and she was, she said, a granddaughter of my Aunt Yentl by her first husband. Hanka was, in fact, not my relative since my Uncle Arn was Yentl's third husband.] (p. 75)

The narrator takes pains to distance himself twice from this woman. First, he reports that she claims to be a relative, without explicitly endorsing that claim. Second, he points out that, even should her geneological assertions prove accurate, she would only be a relative by marriage. Presumably, too, the reader would recognize – or be expected to recognize – Mume Yentl from both the stories in which she is featured and her unique chapter in *Mayn tatns bezdn-shtub*. Yet that same reader would also remember that the central fact of Mume Yentl's autobiographical monologue, and of her life, was her childlessness; "Mume Yentl" was, in large measure, a chronicle of her attempts to bear a child, to obtain from a sufficiently powerful rabbi a sufficiently powerful amulet to assure her pregnancy. That the narrator is not aware of this glaring discrepancy is surprising. Even more surprising is the narrator's mention of "mayn feter Arn" [my Uncle Arn]; we remember the fact, many times restated in *Mayn tatns bezdn-shtub* and even affirmed in the framed fictions, that Yentl's third husband was Singer's Feter Yoysef. Thus, though we are invited to read "Hanka" as autobiographical memoir, we are at the same time precluded from reading it exclusively as such.

Another factor which prevents a strictly historical reading is the introduction of supernatural elements into the narrative. To be more accurate, however, intimations of the supernatural are introduced long before supernatural elements proper. Indeed, the narrator of "Hanka" stands in sharp contrast to those of the old wives' tales, who, at least in their earlier appearances, only gradually yield to supernatural construals of the events they report. By contrast, the present narrator seems all too willing to see supernatural forces at work in occurrences which would not seem to call for their invocation. We are told, for example, how the few fellow-passengers who spoke English aboard the rather seedy Argentine ship en route to Buenos Aires did not speak to him at any great length – a fact attributable to their difference in physical aspect and temperament: "Di manslayt – ale yung, zeks-fisike rizn – hobn geshpilt kriket oder epes an enlekhe shpil oyfn dek un zenen arumgeshvumen in baseyn" [the men – all young, six-foot giants – played cricket or some similar game on deck and swam around in the pool] (p. 74). The narrator, however, is persistent in his inclination to see in his isolation the intervention of hostile demonic forces: "Teyl mol hot zikh mir oysgedukht az kh'bin durkh epes a kishef gevorn a roye-veeyne-nire" [at times it seemed to me that I'd been transformed by some sort of magic into one who sees but isn't seen] (p. 75). When, ensconced in his hotel room in Buenos Aires, the narrator begins to believe that, once again, the fates are arrayed against him, the reader is inclined to dismiss his plaints as those of a hapless *shlimazl*. Would the fates bother to bring on an attack of hay fever (described in embarrassing detail), cause the elevator in his old hotel to break down between floors, or prompt a falling-out among the leaders of the Jewish community which was to delay financing of his provincial tour? The narrator's baffled kvetching undercuts his authority to posit supernatural intervention, which intervention is hardly apparent by independent consideration of the events' evidentiary value.

It would, however, be incorrect to dismiss the narrator's demonic intimations out of hand, for all one is justified in deriving a bit of amusement at his expense. The more credible intimations of the supernatural seem to coalesce around the figure of Hanka, and they are shared by characters significantly less susceptible than the narrator. Khaskl Poliva, for example, an otherwise hardheaded and not overly-sympathetic impresario, also feels ill-luck in the air and identifies it with Hanka. In an interesting reversal of roles, he tells a somewhat sceptical narrator that he'd be better off avoiding her company:

−Zi varft oyf mir a shrek. Zi iz far aykh nisht mazldik.
−Ir gleybt in azoyne zakhn?
−Az m'iz draysik you an impresaryo, muz men darin gleybn.
["She frightens me. She's not lucky for you."
"You believe in such things?"
"When one's been an impresario for thirty years, one has to believe in them."] (p. 83)

Poliva's discomfort is not entirely a matter of intuition: he hadn't ever met Hanka prior to the narrator's arrival at the pier, nor had he ever heard of her, though she claimed to have performed as a dancer at Jewish affairs. An impresario of thirty years' experience cannot reasonably be expected not to have known of a professional performer in his territory.

More unsettingly, Hanka herself encourages, albeit with a measure of ambiguity, the narrator to regard her as not entirely of this world. Though the narrator twice orders substantial meals for her, she leaves the food all but untouched (pp. 76, 79). Her reply to his physical advances is even more explicit:

> Kh'hob mikh gerikht az kh'vel hobn mit Hanka a kurtse afere, ober ven kh'hob zi . . . gepruvt arumnemen, iz ir kerper gevorn vi ayngeshrumpn in mayne hent. Kh'hob zi gekusht un ire lipn zenen geven kalt. Zi hot gezogt: —Kh'kon dikh farshteyn. Du bist a mants-bil. . . . Ober du bist a normaler mentsh, nisht keyn nekroman. Ikh geher tsu a farshnitenem shevet un azoyne zenen nisht keyn materyal far seks.
> [I'd counted on having a short affair with Hanka, but when I tried to embrace her, her body shrank within my hands. I kissed her and her lips were cold. She said: "I can understand you. You're a man. But you're a normal man and not a necromaniac. I belong to a severed tribe and we're no material for sex."] (p. 77)[49]

Has Hanka just warned the narrator that she is a spirit, rather than a living being? Or is this merely her way of telling the narrator that her experiences – we shall shortly hear of her years-long experience walled up in Gentile neighbors' apartment during the Nazi occupation of Warsaw – have deadened her appetites for sex as well as food? The narrator, so willing to see the supernatural in rather trivial events, is here a great deal more cautious; he as the reader, must for the moment suspend judgment.

If improbable and disturbing events seems to settle around Hanka, an incident considerably more improbable and disturbing in volves the narrator's cousin Yekhiyel. While unsure that he is actually related to Hanka, the narrator unambiguously claims blood relation to Yekhiyel, whom he had twice met in pre-War Poland. He is brought to Yekhiyel and his wife by Hanka, who appears one evening unbidden at his bedside and becomes his Beatrice through neighborhoods which grow increasingly decrepit and otherworldly. When the narrator, at first apprehensive of foul play, begins to suspect that his journey is taking him from one world, rather than from one neighborhood, to another, the reader is no longer inclined to laugh: "Perhaps she is a she-devil and will soon reveal her goose feet and pig's snout?" (p. 17).

In the most decayed of these streets, in a shanty of a house, the narrator finds Yekhiyel. After the initial shock, the narrator recognizes the near-catatonic man as his cousin. (Adding to the scene's unreal atmosphere is the realization that Hanka, though she knew her way to this remote location – without telephone and, probably, published address – had apparently never before seen the inhabitants.) Though it takes persistent prodding to evoke even a "sí " or a "no" or a "bueno," there is no doubt in either cousin's mind that they are indeed related. Neither Yekhiyel nor his wife display any emotion at the appearance of guests, one of them a relative; "S'hot gehoykht fun zey mit a midkayt nisht fun der-velt" [They exuded a tiredness not of this world] (p. 86).

The narrator, disoriented by his journey and unable to bring his visit into meaningful focus, begins to doubt the substantiality of both his journey and his guide. Of the former, he says, "Oyb dos iz meglekh, iz shoyn alts meglekh" [If this is possible, everything is possible] (p. 86). In another reversal of roles, Hanka explains that both Yekhiyel and his wife had survived the camps – indeed, had met in Auschwitz. This she offers as straightforward psychological explanation for their lassitude. Yet her phrasing belies the rational consolation which she attempts to offer: "–Yene vos zenen geshtanen bay der shvel fun toyt, blaybn toyte. Ikh bin oykh a toyte. . . . ["Those who stood on the threshold of death remain dead. I'm also dead. . . ."] (p. 86). The question has been shifted from one of the plausibility of Yekhiyel's conduct back to that of his – and Hanka's – physical existence. The narrator, nearly overwhelmed, breaks the spell by admitting aloud that Hanka's very existence is at question and, simultaneously, asking that she call him a cab. This is followed by a break in the narrative, a break in the weather, a break in the lecture tour's ill-luck – all contemporaneous with Hanka's disappearance from the scene.

The narrator's attempts to locate Hanka only reinforce his, and the reader's, uncertainty about her existence: she had avoided telling him her address, or even her last name; Yekhiyel had not called, nor was he listed in the telephone book; no one could make any sense of the landmarks he remembered having passed on his nighttime journey. In themselves, none of these facts – or even all of them in concert – prove supernatural intervention, even in the light of Hanka's disappearance, or of Khaskl Poliva's newly-lifted spirits. They do, however, mediate against a purely naturalistic reading of the incidents. The net effect is, in short, ambiguous, and that ambiguity is fed by the story's generic ambiguities. Just as the quotidian and the supernatural inhabit the same narrated universe, so, too, Hanka, Yekhiyel, and – especially – the Singer-like narrator stand somewhere between reportage and fiction. These interrelations, mutual contingencies and constraints are more complex in "Hanka" than in any of the pieces which precede it; the result is a text less schematically precise than many of the earlier stories with old woman narrators. "Hanka," coda-like, juxtaposes the familiar variables in a text at once more grounded as historical memoir – through, among other devices, the use of characters with historical or quasi-historical analogues – and less hedged as fantastic tale – the character-narrator is actually present at the events in question.

One might expect the story to end without much further ado, its primary rhetorical task accomplished and its central narrative at an end. And, in fact, fewer than two pages of the Yiddish text are devoted to the remainder of the lecture tour. The report of all but the final lecture, for example, reads in its terse entirety: "Alerlay institutsyes hobn gemakht far mir unternemungen. Shulkinder hobn mikh oyfgenumen mit tents un gezang" [All kinds of institutions made arrangements for me. School children greeted me with dance and song] (p. 87). The narrative pace does slow somewhat for the depiction of the narrator's final lecture – which is, in consideration of the largely Communist audience, not on his standard topic, "Literatur un dos ibernatirlekhe" [Literature and the Supernatural], but a reading of humorous pieces. Having successfully parried a number of rather hostile rhetorical questions about the supernatural, the narrator is forced by his final interrogator to address himself to the question directly:

– Hot ir perzenlekh gehat derfarungen fun dem sort? Hot ir a mol gezen a gayst?
Kh'hob geentfert:
– Ale mayne derfarungen zenen geven tsveydaytik; keyn eyne fun zey kon nisht dinen vi evidents; ober nisht gekukt oyf dem vert mayn gloybn in gayster alts shtarker. ["Have you personally had experience of this kind? Have you ever seen a spirit?
I answered, "All of my experiences were ambiguous; not one of

them could serve as evidence. But, nonetheless, my belief in spirits grows even deeper."] (p. 99)

There is, however, a final twist in the story's final paragraph. Unlike Perets' celebrated *kneytsh*,[50] however, which effectively undermines the contentions established in the course of an extended narrative, Singer's *kneytsh* confirms them:

Der oylem hot mir gegbn aploz. Beys kh'hob aropgeboygn dem kop un gedankt, hob ikh derblikt Hankan. . . . Kh'bin gevorn vi farglivert. . . . Kh'hob vider geton a kuk un zi iz gehat farshvundn. Neyn, s'iz geven a halutsinatsye. S'hot alts gedoyert bloyz eyn rege. Ober kh'vel nisht fargesn di dozike rege vi lang kh'vel lebn. [The audience applauded. While I nodded my head in thanks, I caught a glimpse of Hanka. . . . I nearly froze. . . . I looked again and she had disappeared. No, it was a hallucination. It all lasted only a moment. But I won't forget that moment as long as I live.] (p. 88)

Plot confirms what the authorial persona asserts – the ambiguity of supernatural occurrences. This ambiguity reflects the underlying project of the series under discussion. In each, Singer takes a clearly fictional situation, admixes characters grounded in memoir and leaves the reader wondering which set of generic codes and conventions might best be applied to the text.

Beginning, then, with old wives' tales of unproblematic fictiveness, Singer has successively shaded them toward reportage by introducing a recurring narrator; namely her Yentl; supplying her with a quasi-autobiographical personal history; introducing a Singer-like child auditor; and, finally, merging this series with another, more recently-introduced series of narratives with Singer-like adult character-narrators. As with most Singer strategies, these texts have moved from the less to the more radically experimental; it is difficult to see how, within this particular formal progression, fiction might be shaded more energetically toward reportage. In recent years, Singer has devoted his efforts toward another generic experiment – shading the interview toward fiction. It is to Singer's interviews which we turn in the next, and final, chapter.

Chapter 4

Reportage as Fiction, II: The Interview as Fictional Genre

¿Que es la vida? Una illusión, una sombra, una ficción . . .[1]

Isaac Bashevis Singer has, as we have seen, devised and experimented with a rather large number of strategies both to undermine the fictiveness of his ostensibly fictional writings and to suggest that his nonfictional writings might best be apprehended as near-fictions. There is, moreover, a general movement in his work from the less to the more radically experimental. Accordingly, it is not surprising that Singer would at last attempt to fictionalize a type of writing the entire raison d'etre of which is its claim to literal historicity – the interview. I propose to discuss here how Singer manipulates both interview and interviewer in an attempt to make of a critical format a literary form.

The first thing which strikes one when considering Singer's interviews is their number, both in absolute terms and in relation to both his other works and to the works about his person and oeuvre. No exact enumeration is practicably possible, since the number of published and broadcast interviews must surely be in the hundreds. Bryer and Rockwell's bibliography of "Isaac Bashevis Singer in English,"[2] reasonably complete through 1 July 1968, records some thirty-two interviews; in addition to these, I have located another twenty-six. They appear in scholarly journals (*Criticism, Contemporary Literature, Diacritics*, to name just three), little magazines (*The Handle, Nimrod*), mass-circulation glossies (*Esquire, Vogue*), newspapers major (the *New York Times, Washington Post, Miami Herald*) and decidedly minor (the *Detroit Jewish News*). There are already more English-language interviews in print than short stories. Moreover, the interview is the ony genre in which Singer's voice is originally in English (save a handful of stories for children). Nor are the isoglosses of Singer's spiritual landscape clearly delineated: articles on Singer are almost invariably derived from information supplied by the author, rather than from first-hand research. Thus, for example, Singer provided the often-repeated data for Buchen's biography,[3] the biographical details for Paul Kresh's *Magician of West 86th Street,*[4] the background for articles on him in the popular press. (The mechanics of syndication assist this blurring of distinctions between interview and reportage: not only do the *New York Times* Press Service and API distribute Singer's interviews for republication; they also write news articles based upon and circulated almost simultaneously with the underlying interviews.)[5]

Kresh observed the (admittedly large) number of interviews granted by Singer for broadcast or publication on a single day – 5 October 1978: "As the day wore on, Isaac gave out dozens of interviews to television, radio, newspaper, and magazine reporters. . . . Dick Cavett taped a new introduction to the interview he had done with Isaac during the summer, and the show was run on educational television. Wherever one switched on the dial, there was Isaac. . . ." (pp. 396-97). This underscores not only the number of interviews granted by Singer, but also his accessibility for interviews. Until receiving the Nobel Prize, Singer elected to list his telephone number in the Manhattan directory; his address and telephone number in Miami are still listed. Indeed, Morris Lurie prefaces his interview with Singer with a report of an earlier conversation with Herbert Gold, who told Lurie that "Certainly you must see Singer. Oh, he'll see you. He sees everyone."[6] Nor is Singer grudging with his time: many interviewers are invited to dine with him or to return for follow-up interviews, and Singer permitted Richard Burgin to interview him "over the course of more than two years" for a total of "fifty or so taped interviews."[7]

Finally, though the interview is – initially at least – a spoken genre, Singer engages in its written counterpart by furnishing answers to questions addressed to him by curious readers. Though Kresh exaggerates in observing the "Isaac reads them all, answers them all" (313), the surprising aspect of these interviews-by-correspondence is not that Singer is erratic in his replies, but that he replies at all.[8] This willingness, indeed eagerness, to engage his would-be interviewers stems, I would assert, not from personal malleability, but from authorial self-interest; his colloquants to not as much succeed in pinning Singer down for interviews as much as Singer succeeds in attracting and, as we shall examine, manipulating his interviewers to his own ends.

These ends are, despite Singer's profoundly self-avowed concern with his own financial well-being (see, for example, "What's in It for Me?"),[9] not in this case pecuniary: he rarely and reluctantly discusses either works-in-progress or works being published, unlike those customarily-reticent authors (Kurt Vonnegut, Philip Roth) who appear in print only to promote their current production. In fact, he is rather more inclined to answer questions about himself than about his works. Withal, there is little doubt that Singer, and not his interviewers, is the controlling intellect and, as it were, author of his many interviews.

Kresh reports how, on 20 July 1976, Singer chose to speak only of the report that an American spacecraft, Viking I, had landed safely on Mars: "All afternoon he can talk of nothing else but the news from Mars. A fellow writing an article for a literary magazine arrives for an interview. Isaac virtually ignores his questions . . . and will talk to him only of Mars" (p. 108). More frequently, Singer steers conversation not away from, but toward, himself. Kresh accurately observes that, in an interview with Philip Roth on Bruno Schulz accompanying the republication of Schulz's *Street of Crocodiles* in English, "the subject was supposed to be Bruno Schulz but as the conversation between Isaac and Roth proceded the subject veered closer and closer to Isaac and further from Schulz."[10]

Singer's non-responsiveness is not always a matter of omission, however; he has, for example, more than once posed and immediately answered his own questions or, as in an interview with Marshall Breger and Bob Barnhart, volunteered answers to entirely unasked questions. After the interviewers announce the conclusion of their interview with "I guess that's about it," Singer himself opens a new line of discussion: "Let me add to you that I am a sincere vegetarian. You may be interested to know that. . . ."[11] Similarly, Singer answers Grace Farrell Lee's question about the ecumenical import of human anguish in the face of a silent God animatedly and at some length but then slips laterally into a none-too-subtle denunciation of carnivorism: "Not only does anguish unite the Jewish and the non-Jewish, but the man and the animal. It does not express it in words, but when an animal screams it is the same scream as that of a human being. The animal also asks God, why have you forsaken us?"[12] Reena Sara Ribalow, an unusually tenacious interviewer clearly undiverted by Singer's considerable personal charm, echoes the frustration of many of the better-prepared interviewers: "I had the impression that he was talking more to himself than to me."[13] But Ribalow misconstrues Singer's non-responsiveness as indifference toward his audience: not the interviewer, but the eventual reader or viewer, is Singer's intended audience; for his or her part, the interviewer is only its occasion or proximate cause, never its author. This is the motivation of Singer's several devices to undercut the authority of the interviewer.

Inevitably, the role of the interviewer must carry with it a certain assumption of authority. To the extent that he cannot entirely do away with an interrogator and still fulfill the formal criteria of the interview as genre, Singer himself assumes – or, rather, usurps – that role. "Naturally," Singer confides to Grace Farrell Lee, "I'm curious. As a matter of fact when a person comes to interview me I interview this person, because I'm just as curious about this person as this person is curious about me."[14] At times Singer attributes his reversal of roles not to curiosity, but to a professional data-gathering upon which to base later fictions: "I begin . . . the moment a man comes to me or a woman to ask them . . . how do you live? Are you married and if you are not do you have a boyfriend or a girlfriend? I get them to tell stories."[15] "Those who come to ask questions are surprised to find themselves being interviewed instead. 'I take from everything,' he says."[16]

If Singer's textual strategies work to claim the interview as his own, he also stakes a more conventional claim of ownership. In a relatively early interview, David Andersen acknowledges

Singer's role as (self-suggested?) revisor: "We are grateful to Mr. Singer for kindly consenting to check the manuscript for accuracy."[17] In later interviews the initiative is less ambiguously ascribable: "In the end," reports B. Midwood in *Esquire*, "Mr. Singer walked us to the door, chattering all the way, still amazed and agitated, and then suddenly he turned to me and in a very serious tone reminded me of a request he had made earlier – to show him the manuscript of the interview before publication."[18] The recently published interviews with Richard Burgin are jointly copyrighted; Isaac Bashevis Singer's name comes first.

I have elsewhere discussed how packaging may function as determinant of textual ontology.[19] On the one hand, the texts we have been considering have the formal attributes of the interview, e.g., question-and-answer format and generic tag as title ("An Interview with, . . . "A Conversation with. . . ."). On the other hand, by claiming authorship of his interviews and by drawing the reader's attention to that claim, Singer effectively undermines their generic stability. This process is often abetted by the titles of Singer's interviews, which, with increasing frequency, have been appearing not only without conventional generic tagging (e.g., "Isaac Bashevis Singer Talks About . . . Everything"),[20] but often entirely without reference in the title to the text as transcribed oral performance (e.g., "The Magician of West 86th Street," "His Demons Are Real," "The Story of Isaac").[21]

A number of Singer's interviewers have further confused generic expectations and nudged the interview into a subgenre of sorts – the third-person interview. Here, the focus is on the temporal or spatial specifics of the conversation (a student dining commons in G. F. Lee's "Stewed Prunes and Rice Pudding," for example, or a dairy restaurant in Cathy Lynn Grossman's "The Story of Isaac")[22] and the presence, impressions, and prose style of the interviewer. Typically, the texts move between third-person summary and first-person quotation with transitional passages of physical description of Singer, his apartment, secretary, writing desk, etc. Here the motivation transparently is a desire to share the spotlight, both as object and controlling intelligence, with a famous and accessible author. The result, however, is not an interplay of intelligences of an objective test of Singer's reportorial reliability, for one of his third-person interviewers possesses much in the way of independent knowledge of Singer's oeuvre, but rather the interposition of yet another cognitive layer between speech act and written text.

Contrary to what one assumes the intentions of their authors to have been, the third-person interviews no more belong to their interviewers than do their first-person correlates. For one thing, Singer's verbal acumen far outstrips that of his interviewers, foregrounding his contribution to what must, in some sense, be considered a collectively-authored text. (In general, the first-person interviewers come away less scathed due to the clearer delineation of function between questioner and informant.) Moreover, the similarity in Singer's replies – whether cited or summarized – establishes a series of intertextualities which bind interview to interview through their common element – Isaac Singer.

An important if unsought result of embedding interviews in a discursive prose context is further to isolate them from their original context as speech acts. Thus the texts of Singer's interviews do not stand in the same relationship to their original performance as do, say, the texts of plays to their eventual mise-en-scène: it is not just that the reader apprehends the interview in written form – for the viewer of Singer's televised interviews does witness a verbal performance – but, rather, that the interviews in whatever mode do not refer back to their original instrumental contexts but are offered the reader for use as independent texts. And this is precisely wherein the literariness of texts inheres. As John Ellis writes: "Literary texts are defined as those that are used by the society in such a way that *the text is not taken as specifically relevant to the immediate context of its origin*."[23] This is the process to which Richard Burgin was reacting intuitively when he remarked that "I quickly learned that Isaac Singer's conversation . . . was itself a kind of literature."[24]

"In an important way," Ellis continues, "texts are made into literature by the community by their authors. . . . Many are offered; but few are chosen" (p. 47). It is clear that the community has made such a choice on a number of occasions. Ralph L. Woods, for example, compiler of a popular gift book, *The Joy of Jewish Humor*,[25] reprints an edited excerpt of an interview with Singer and Israel Shenker from the *New York Times*,[26] setting it in apposition to literary and, in part, canonized texts; it is the only such transcription from an oral source, directly precedes a quotation from the Talmud, and is one of the relatevely few texts of the post-Enlightenment period. For their part, the editors of the *New York Times*, apparently upset by the necessity of reporting the grisly details of the 911 suicides (as they were then thought to have been) in Jonestown, Guyana, chose to reprint "the quiet reflections of Isaac Bashevis Singer," a portion of an earlier interview, "by way of antidote to counteract the poison of the bad news from Jonestown."[27] Here, Singer's "quiet reflections" were used in a context entirely unrelated to that of their genesis, i.e. as literary texts. Yet one should not overstate the case: it is precisely because Singer's remarks were those of an historic person, delivered on a recorded date, and originally published in a non-literary medium (i.e. the *New York Times*) that they were deemed suitable for publication in the *Times'* news pages. My point is not that these interviews, by virtue of the use to which they have been put, have attained unambiguous literary status but rather that they are ontologically unstable and function both as primary and secondary texts.

Leaving the question of the texts' ontological status momentarily aside, we shall have to inquire why Singer labored so hard to assert his authorship of his interviews. It is not to give truer or more reliable comments about his oeuvre, since he avoids, for the most part, comment on his work in favor of biographical anecdote. But it is more than authorial reticence which compels Singer to keep his silence on matters of interpretation, especially considering the volubility with which he announces his silence. Rather, Singer asserts claims of ownership only to disavow anyone's privileged access to a literary text; they are the property of the community which uses them: somewhat paradoxically perhaps, he invokes the right of authorship to release his readership from the constraints of normative reading.

In so doing, he develops a number of potentially contradictory theories of the text. One such theory holds that texts — whether all texts or only certain ones is left unresolved — are plurisignificant; they admit of no normative reading not because of the lack of arbiting authority but, rather, because texts may mean different things at the same time. Accordingly, Singer parries Burgin's probings on the reality of metempsychosis in *The Manor* (*Der hoyf*):

> Burgin: And what did you intend?
> Singer: Well I would say that when I write about such things, I always make them ambiguous.[28]

At times, Singer implies that the ambiguity inheres in his own ambivalent feelings about the reality of the supernatural, at times—and more interestingly—in the basic nature of literary texts.

In an anecdote he repeats with some frequency, Singer shows himself willing to countenance interpretations based upon the text's organization, rather than upon authorial intentionality. "After I published *The Magician of Lublin*," he tells David Andersen, "I got a telephone call from a psychoanalyst, and he said, 'I loved the way you made your hero go back to his mother's womb.' It never occurred to me for a moment that the Magician of Lublin went back to his mother's womb, but I said to him, 'Once a story is ritten it's not anymore my private property, and you are as entitled to find your interpretation as I am.'"[29] Though one may regret the extent of Singer's critical laissez-faire—surely there are readings which are objectively incorrect—one must applaud how he sanctions the critic's right to notice aspects of his stories of which he, their author, had previously been ignorant. Singer seems intuitively to have located the process by which texts become literary texts: "I think the moment you have published a book, it's not any more your private property. . . . It belongs already in a way to humanity."[30]

Singer has just summarized both the classical anti-intentionalist argument of Wimsatt and Beardsley, i.e. that "the design or intention of the author is neither available nor desirable as a standard for judging . . . a work of literary art,"[31] as well as Ellis' more fundamental rejection of biographical data, i.e. that to consider a work in the context of its origins "returns," in Ellis' words, "the text to its former status, and reverses the process of its becoming a literary text" (p. 113). Singer's interviewers, however, find these assertions difficult to credit, both as critical precepts and as expression of Singer's own predilections. The following exchange between Singer and Richard Burgin is unusual only in the extent of the interviewer's tenacity:

> Burgin: What you say seems true to me. But if, let's say, you had a chance to meet Tolstoy,, wouldn't that interest or excite you?
> Singer: The truth is if Tolstoy would live across the street, I wouldn't go to see him. I would rather read what he writes.
> Burgin: You wouldn't be curious to meet him face-to-face?
> Singer: Not really. . . . I've heard people make such a fuss about it, that Shakespeare did not write his plays. . . . What is the difference who wrote them?
> Burgin: And you wouldn't be curious to meet Shakespeare?
> Singer: Not at all. Not for a moment. You see, I don't care if his work was written by Bacon or Shakespeare. If someone would tell me that Tolstoy didn't write his books I also wouldn't care, I would be just as happy. This interest in the artist has become the idolatry of our time.[32]

My point, however, is not to suggest that Singer's interviews be considered without reference to the autobiographical assertions they contain – the interview is generically predicated upon a claim to literal historicity and to the utility of the information it provides – but rather to reiterate from a somewhat different perspective Singer's attempt to undermine the generic expectations associated with the interview format. And, indeed, we have seen how he assumed authorship of the interviews so readily granted, effectively suppressing their original status as direct oral performance.

I should like to make two additional observations about Singer's interviews before turning to the actual biographical data they purport to convey. The first is that the reader is encouraged to view a given interview as part of the total corpus of Singer interviews. To an extent, of course, this is inevitable: the reader/viewer sufficiently interested in Isaac Bashevis Singer to read or watch one interview is, I suspect, likely to have come across a number – perhaps a sizeable number – of other such interviews. (Nearly a dozen interviews with Singer have been published by the *New York Times*, for example, in as many years.) Yet whereas Singer's interviewers sometimes feel compelled to offer apologies for publishing yet another interview with the same subject (Andersen prefaces his interview with both an apology and a bibliography: "This transcript complements a number of other published interviews which the reader will find of interest"),[33] Singer himself draws the reader's attention both to the number of interviews he grants and to the intertextualities which naturally arise from this interview explosion. Speaking with a reporter for the *Washington Post,* for example, he notes that "Before the Prize, of course, I did not give every week fifty interviews, but it's more or less the same. . . .[34] And, prefacing his answer to Laurie Colwin's question about the conditions he needs to write a story, Singer remarks that "I have said this a few times before, and I can repeat it."[35]

The second point is that strong intertextualities actually exist beyond those determined by the identity of format and interviewee, and by the allusions to other interviews made by Singer and his questioners. That is, the texts themselves contain cross references, leitmotifs, and other allusive devices. A short catalogue should suffice to describe the more important intertextual modalities. Singer's most striking strategy is an almost word-for-word repetition of answers to a number of recurring questions. (Of course, interviewers, many of whom have only the slightest acquaintance with Singer's works, even in translation, often prefer the "research" of seeing what questions have already been asked and, quite possibly seeing what questions have elicited the most striking replies.) "Three Conditions to Write a Story" has even acquired a stable title known to interviewer, informant, and reader alike.[36] The same is true for "Ten Reasons Why I Write for Children," originally a National book Award speech but since reprinted both as an interview and discrete essay.[37] This flexibility of form, one should note, undermines the piece's ontological stability while emphasizing its intertextualities.

The careful reader will also note the reappearance of a considerable number of proverbs and proverb-like utterances from interview to interview. To Sanford Pinsker Singer remarks that "The moment a writer has written one line he is already not a free man because the second line depends already upon the first one";[38] speaking with Richard Burgin, he cites the folkloristic subtext: "They say in Yiddish, 'If you have said Aleph you have to say Beth.'"[39] And an interview with Singer would hardly be complete without his telling the interviewer, bidden or unbidden, that he is not a "sociologizer" or "psychologizer."

There are, finally, a number of verbal leitmotifs which, while used to refer to diverse objects, bind the texts in which they appear to other texts with the same leitmotif. A single example should suffice – the word *amnesia*, an otherwise fairly uncommon word which appears in a great variety of contexts. In one such context, Singer abjures Morton Reichek and his readers not to denegrate the last two thousand years of Jewish experience and the cultural products which it produced: "Forgetting the Exile would mean going into such an amnesia which would kill the Jewish spirit; so all these people who speak about the Exile, as something which should be forgotten are really senseless people, complete idiots."[40] Lamenting his inability to remember his dreams upon waking, Singer says to Richard Burgin: "There is a certain amnesia about dreams."[41] And speaking with Sander Gilman about the persistence of Jewish collective memory: "We are a very restless people and as I once said: we Jews suffer from many diseases, but amnesia is not one of them."[42] Though I have been unable to locate the earlier appearance of this statement to which Singer refers, it is interesting to see how Singer himself alerts the reader to the intertextual possibilities of his reply. A fourth appearance of *amnesia* – and the most interesting – will be discussed later in this chapter.

The geniality and formal accessibility of Singer's interviews belie the radical reorientation of generic experimentations which they undertake to produce. We have already examined how the reader has been encouraged, by strategies both textual and extratextual, to overlook two distinct but related generic attributes. First, Singer offers these interviews not as biographical documents but as literary texts – that is, as utterances not dependent upon a reconstruction of their original instrumental contexts for proper apprehension. Second, the insistent intertextualities which we have begun to explore undermine the descreteness of a given interview and encourage the reader to view it as a segmnet of a single, far larger, and as yet unfinished, work.

Yet any attempt on the part of a single author definitively to reorient the readers' generic expectations is doomed to failure or, at best, to unstable success: the combined effects of structure and convention are not easily overcome. Inevitably, the reader will frame Singer's interviews together with the balance of interviews previously encountered, and bring to them those expectations fostered by the genre as a whole. Primary among these expectations is the interview's claim to literal historicity. Indeed, this is its presumed raison d'être as well as the motivation of its various structural components. Thus, for example, the practical give-and-take of the first-person format effectively precludes Singer from assuming sole authorship of an interview, for all that his is recognizably its controlling intellect. And any situation comprised of interrogator and interrogated necessarily casts an associational net wider than that of the literary interview alone; one is reminded of policeman and detainee, personnel officer and job applicant, dissertation committee and doctoral candidate. Finally, experience teaches that each interview is a discrete performance – David Frost and Daniel Schorr do not elicit the same manner of response from Richard Nixon.

Having established the interview as a genre on the margin of literariness, Singer undertakes to create for and of himself a persona on the margin of fictiveness. Moreover, Singer's persona-building is predicated on the readers' awareness of and, in an important sense, participation in, the author's sleight-of-hand. This is achieved through the public manipulation of a number of discrete though interrelated intertextual modalities. In one such manipulation, Singer challenges the reader to accept the simultaneous veracity of two or more contradictory assertions from the corpus of interviews. In another, he asserts the literal historicity of an incident known by even the casual reader to be inaccurate. Thus we have both text-to-text and text-to-life discrepancies, which we shall examine in turn.

We have discussed how Singer's replies often tend to form near-identical clusters, both in content and linguistic surface. An initial function of this clustering is, as I have asserted, the establishment of a meta-interview of which each indivicually published conversation is but a segment. Thus, for example, Singer is fond of retelling how his first words in English were "take a chair":

B: *How much English did you know when you came here?*
S: Nothing. I knew three words: "Take a chair." But there was only

one camping chair in my furnished room and no one visited me there.[43]

. . . .

When he arrived in this country, Singer could only speak three words of English . . . I ask him what those three words of English were he brought to this country, and he speaks this phrase: "Take a chair." On this Sunday afternoon at 4 p.m., he cannot explain this. I'm glad.[44]

(We might note in passing how Cathy Lynn Grossman, Singer's colloquant in the second citation, apparently cued by a quotable anecdote from an earlier interview, cued Singer in turn by asking him to name his first three English words; Singer complied, bringing the process full circle and emphasizing thereby the self-referentiality of reported incident.) How is the reader to reconcile these accounts with an equally engaging one Singer related to Philip Roth in the course of an interview on Bruno Schulz:

I came here and saw that everybody speaks English. I mean, there was a Hadassah meeting, and so I went and expected to hear Yiddish. But I came in and there was sitting about two hundred women and I heard one word, "delicious, delicious, delicious." I didn't know which it was, but it wasn't Yiddish. I didn't know what they gave them to eat, but two hundred women were sitting and saying "delicious." By the way, this was the first English word I learned.[45]

In a strictly literal sense, both assertions cannot possibly be accurate: both "take a chair" and "delicious" vie for the same space and can only be reconciled by considering one, the other, or both as a lie. And at least one prominent Yiddish literary scholar – in critical synecdoche for the community he represents – has accused Singer of simple dishonesty in his memoiristic reportage. Taken not as reportage but as what Barbara Herrnstein Smith terms "fictive discourse,"[46] however, the anecdotes serve complementary, rather than contradictory, functions. Each purports to chronicle a situation similar in aspect, as well as in import. Singer, newly arrived in a country both alien and alienating, found himself isolated not as much from a broader society then but dimly apprehended as from the society of Eastern European Jews who immigrated to America not appreciably earlier than he. His linguistic isolation is conjoined in the first incident with the barrenness of his furnished room and foregrounded in the second by an awareness of his presumably unique male presence at the meeting of a women's society – one wonders, by the way, how Singer contrived to gain admittance to a Hadassah meeting in the first place. As reportage, "take a chair" and "delicious" cannot both have been his first English words, but either might appropriately have been. More radically, Singer suggests that, within a fictional frame, not either but *both* might have been his first words. By a kind of algebraic logic wherein two quantities equal to the same quantity are equal to one another, Singer posits multiple personal histories disparate in detail but identical in import.

What is impossible in life, Singer suggests, is possible in fiction – hardly a revolutionary assertion. But the process by which Singer moves personal history toward fiction is both subtle and unusual. On the one hand, formal conventions and the generic expectations which they engender would have the reader accept the literal historicity of Singer's interviews. On the other hand, the factual situations which they purport to chronicle may only successfully be naturalized as fiction. And since fictiveness inheres, as I have argued after Ellis and Herrnstein Smith, not within a text but within its readership, the extent to which that readership accepts these multiple personal histories as noncontradictory is a measure of Singer's success in the making of fictions. Thus the reader's task is not merely to perceive Singer's ontological play but to participate with him in the game.

The mode of fiction-building we have been discussing is predicated on a perceived discrepancy between two texts and derives its authority from the texts alone, since a reader cannot be presumed to have privileged access to the biographical details which they purport to chronicle. Singer also employs a related strategy based on a different set of discrepancies – those between interview text and the readers' independent memory of public events in Singer's literary career. This is hardly arcane knowledge: though a regular, engaged reader of the *Jewish Daily Forward* – is there any other kind of *Forverts* reader? – might fail to remember the precise details of a half-century's publishing history, its major contours are certainly shared *Kulturgut*.

The emotional common denominator of the anecdotes Singer sets in this period is his linguistic alienation as an immigrant Yiddish writer and its attendant physical, psychological, and financial burdens. Unlike the accounts of his first English words, which are often told with a measure of wry detachment, the episodes hinging on text-life descrepancies tend to be utterly serious even when positive in outcome. To be sure, the stakes – here personal and professional survival – are also greater. Repeatedly, even obsessively, Singer refers to a nearly decade-long writer's block occasioned, at least in biographical retrospect, by his lack of confidence in the ability of Yiddish to sustain itself in America as a bearer of an important literary culture and to sustain him as a producer of that culture. Thus in 1963 Singer tells Joel Blocker and Richard Elman:

> When I came to this country I lived through a terrible disappointment. I felt then – more than I believe now – that Yiddish had no future in this country. In Poland, Yiddish was very much alive when I left. When I came here it seemed to me that Yiddish was finished: it was very depressing. The result was that for five or six or maybe seven years I couldn't write a word. Not only didn't I publish anything in those years, but writing became so difficult a chore that my grammar was affected. . . . I shouldn't even have tried to write anything, but I did try again and again, without success. The novel I tried to write I eventually threw away. In later years when I looked at it I was startled to find that it was the work of an illiterate man – and this was after I had written *Satan in Goray*. . . . It was a real case of amnesia.[47]

We have seen that Singer's way with literary experimentation is to test a convention or generic expectation with increasingly radical departures from the norm. In later interviews, Singer remains true to tendency by retelling this episode in essentially unchanged form – but with each retelling, the duration of his recalled writer's block increases. Five years after the interview with Blocker and Elman, Singer revised the episode in a conversation with Irving Buchen later rewritten in the third person and incorporated into an authorized account of Singer's "Life and Works."[48] Singer married his present wife, Alma, in 1940, after which the couple moved to an apartment in Brooklyn:

Little by little, he began to write again. Long works fell apart in his hands, but he was able to make some progress with short stories. The first story that promised to flourish began: "I am the Primeval Snake, the Evil One, Satan. The cabala refers to me as Samael and the Jews sometimes call me merely, "that one."[49]

The quotation, unidentified by Buchen, is from "Der khurbn fun Kreshev" [The Destruction of Kreshev], published in 1943 but written a year earlier.[50] And ten years after the interview with Buchen, Singer adds yet another three years to his period of inactivity. "Between 1935 and 1945," he tells Richard Burgin, "I accomplished nothing. Then I suddenly began to write 'The Family Moskat' for the Forward."[51] Whether the increasing availability of reliable bibliographical data in English on singer's oeuvre will provoke more guarded answers from him in the future or whether, as I suspect, Singer will welcome the broader anglophone readership into this particular game remains to be seen. What is however, beyond doubt is that the Yiddish readership knows the entire story of Singer's writer's block to be a fiction.

In fact, the years following Singer's arrival in America were ones of unprecedented creative activity. In the course of 1935, for example, Singer began to publish a major novel, *Der zindiker meshiekh* [The Sinning Messiah], in the *Forverts*. And 1936, far from being a year of inactivity, saw the publication of the largest number of items in a single year thus far, including one short story in an important literary journal and, in the *Forverts*, four short stories, two sketches, five book reviews, and the completion of his novel. In all, Singer published a total of twenty-six periodical contributions in the decade between his literary debut and his emigration to the United States: the second twenty-six took him less than half the time. By the end of 1943, Singer had published no fewer than 285 pieces in the Yiddish periodical press.[52]

To what should we attribute this remarkable discrepancy between report and reality? Surely not to amnesia, though *amnesia* might well alert the attentive reader to the self-consciousness of Singer's strategy. First, we have seen earlier how the word functions in an intertextual matrix, placing the interview in apposition with other interview texts, rather than with life unmediated. Second, the word serves as clue to the fictivenes of the entire episode. "We Jews suffer from many diseases," Singer tells Sander L. Gilman at the conclusion of an interview, "but amnesia is not one of them."[53] This, in turn, invites one of two possible reactions: wonderment at his *khutspe* in recasting personal history so radically or collaboration in the game of writing reportage as fiction. As I have argued, the two reactions are not mutually exclusive. To the contrary, Singer only succeeds insofar as the reader remains aware of the discrepancies between the facts and fictions of his oeuvre, and, despite the awareness of these discrepancies, chooses to naturalize the texts both as fiction and as reportage, and both simultaneously. Only by exploiting the readers' inherent function as determiners of textual ontology can Singer reconcile his fear of fiction with the pleasures and usefulness of creating fictions.[54]

Singer must share this belief, for in recent interviews he has shown an increasing tendency to undercut his own authority as informant. One sign of a mature genre is its susceptibility to reflexive experimentation. This is only possible when author and reader share a tradition of generic expectations and when the genre itself has become stable in its conventions. That Singer acknowledges the primacy of virtual over literal historicity is delightfully apparent in the prefatory comments to his interview with Paul Rosenblatt and Gene Koppel:

Rosenblatt: There are several questions that we have been thinking about – general questions, some of which I am sure you have been asked before.
Singer: All right. I will try to give you different answers.[55]

Chapter 5

Coda

What critical tradition there is has tended to view Isaac Bashevis Singer as a "passionate primitive,"[1] a "story-teller,"[2] a "magician"[3] — certainly not as the self-conscious modernist his works proclaim him to be. Singer has collaborated with his critics in establishing these critical commonplaces; indeed, he has frequently been their instigator. In "Why I Write for Children," for example, we reads that "They don't try to understand Kafka or *Finnegans Wake*; they still believe in . . . angels, devils, witches, goblins, . . . and other such obsolete stuff."[4] Whereas it is certainly true that Singer dislikes the rowdier works of the avant-garde and, in his own oeuvre, avoids works which announce their experimental nature too overtly, this is not the product of an antipathy toward formal experimentation. Quite the contrary: Singer's complaint with the avant-garde is that it ignores the formal possibilities of working with, and against, inherited genres.

Throughout his career, Singer's experimentation has centered on questions of genre: nearly every one of the works signed Yitskhok Bashevis, and a large portion of those signed Yitskhok Varshavski or D. Segal, bears a generic tag as subtitle. Even the comparatively modest subset of works examined in the course of this study include such generic tags as "portret" [portrait], "skitse" [sketch], "kharakter-portret" [character portrait], "historisher roman" [historical novel], "khronik" [chronicle], "shpas" [joke, jest], "novele" [novella, *Novelle*], "dertseylung" [(short) story], "bobe-

mayse" [old wives' tale]. This might, not without some justification, be seen as part of a general attempt on the part of recent
Yiddish writers to broaden the scope of Yiddish literature from
the chapbook romances, didactic novels, and humorous
monologues which dominated the literary output of the period
preceding the First World War. (Especially in the United States,
and especially in the domain of poetry, it is far easier to locate
a vilanelle, a rondo, an aubade, a sonnet, or a sestina than it is
to find a serious writer willing to sign his or her name to, say,
a narrative poem in the manner of Perets.) On the other hand,
Singer's generic tags are those already familiar to the readership
of the newspapers and journals in which his works appear, rather
than those appropriated from other literary traditions. The
readers' familiarity with these forms permits Singer to manipulate
generic norms to further his particular project with a measure
of assurance that his readership will correctly apprehend this
public play.

The project itself is as straightforward as the strategies
employed to further it are diverse and complex: Singer seeks, by
means textual and contextual, to blur distinctions between fiction and reportage.

Early in his career this consisted, by and large, of selecting
genres which themselves lie on the border of fiction and reportage. At a somewhat later stage, Singer undertook to burden single
texts with simultaneous or consecutive allusions to a number of
inherited genres — some clearly fictive, some clearly reportorial,
others themselves of ambiguous fictional status. During the
decade-long hiatus in Singer's writing of fiction, he developed a
number of related strategies designed to move reportage toward
fiction; these were ascribed to one or another of his pseudonymous personas. More recently, Singer has experimented with
recurring narrative situations in a series of texts of increasingly
ambiguous fictional status. Finally, he has attempted to make of
the interview — a critical format the raison d'être of which is its
claim to literal historicity — a literary form partaking of elements
both fictional and reportorial. This study has attempted to deal
with each in turn, and in some detail.

There are, to be sure, numerous patterns to be found in the
corpus of an author as accomplished and prolific as Singer; I do

not claim to have found the key to his oeuvre – indeed, would not, for reasons both theoretical and empirical, concede that such a key exists to be found. Moreover, this investigation, which has focused largely upon Singer's own works, would be complemented by a study of the broader literary traditions – Yiddish, Western European (especially Germanic), and Hebraic – of which Singer's works are a part. Such a comparative view is nearly always a desideratum – all the more so with Singer, whose works depend in uncommon measure upon a readership familiar with the generic norms informing his playfully subversive texts. But, by having considered a number of texts which have thus far received little or no critical attention, and by having located a persistent pattern of generic mixing in them, I hope to have made a contribution.

Notes

Preface

1. The most important of these were published in *Shriftn fun der katedre far yidisher kultur ba der alukrainisher visnshaftlekher akademye — literarishe un filologishe sektsyes* (Kiev: Kultur-lige, 1928 ff.) and in its Byelorussian counterpart, *Tsaytshrift far yidisher geshikhte, demografye un ekonomik, literatur-forshung, shprakh-visnshaft un etnografye* (Minsk: Melukhe-farlag fun vaysrusishn s.s.r., 1927–34). These were followed by sporadic publications through the late 1930's, when Yiddish scholarly activities were suppressed.

2. Among the publications devoted, wholly or in substantial measure, to literary scholarship were *Filologishe shriftn fun Yivo* (Warsaw, 1926–28), *Pinkes . . . far yidisher literatur-geshikhte, shprakhforshung, folklor un biblyografye* (New York, 1929), *Yivobleter* (Vilna/New York, 1931–date), *Shriftn fun Amopteyl* (New York, 1938). The titles of YIVO publications, their editorial boards and policies, and their place of publication vary, sometimes from issue to issue; one does best to consult the shelf list at the YIVO Library in New York.

3. On Yiddish literary and cultural life in America during this period, see Irving Howe, *World of Our Fathers* (New York: Harcourt, 1976); on the same period in Poland, see Lucjan Dobroszycki and Barbara Kirshenblatt-Gimblett, *Image Before My Eyes* (New York: Schocken, 1977). Both books contain extensive bibliographies.

4. An interesting exception is Leo Wiener, *The History of Yiddish Literature in the Nineteenth Century* (1899; rpt. New York: Hermon, 1972), written by a member of the Slavic faculty at Harvard University.

5. Thus, for example, Zalmen Reyzen's four-volume *Leksikon fun der yidisher literatur, prese un filologye* (2nd edn.; Vilna: Vilner farlag fun B. Kletskin, 1929) has no entry for Singer.

6. Isaac Bashevis Singer, "Gimpel the Fool," tr. Saul Bellow, *Partisan Review*, 20 (May 1953, 300–13. For bibliographical details of the original Yiddish publication, see p. 144, n. 8.

7. These include Irving Buchen, *Isaac Bashevis Singer and the Eternal Past* (New York: New York Univ. Press, 1968); Irving Malin, *Isaac Bashevis Singer* (New York: Ungar, 1972); Edward Alexander, *Isaac Bashevis Singer*, TWAS 582 *(Boston: Twayne, 1980); Paul Kresh, Isaac Bashevis Singer: The Magician of West 86th Street* (New York: Dial, 1979); Ben Siegel, *Isaac Bashevis Singer* (Minneapolis: Univ. of Minnesota Press, 1969); Marcia Allentuck, ed., *The Achievement of Isaac Bashevis Singer* (Carbondale: Southern Illinois Univ. Press, 1969); and Irving Malin, ed., *Critical Views of Isaac Bashevis Singer* (New York: New York Univ. Press, 1969).

8. The *MLA International Bibliography* records thirty-three articles on Singer for the years 1976–80; only a single article demonstrates linguistic competence in Yiddish.

9. *DAI* records five doctoral dissertations on Singer for the years 1978–81; none demonstrates linguistic competence in Yiddish.

10. On the inadvisability of relying upon English translations of Singer's works, see Chone Shmeruk, "The Use of Monologue as a Narrative Technique in the Stories of Isaac Bashevis Singer," in *Der shpigl un andere dertseylungen*, ed. Chone Shmeruk ([Tel-Aviv]: Hebreisher universitet in Yerusholayim, Yidish-opteylung un Komitet far yidisher fulture in Yisroel, 1975), pp. v–ix, xxxiv–xxxv (n. 35), et passim. See also Leonard Prager's comparison of the endings of "Der kurtser fraytik" [Short Friday] in English and Yiddish; "Ironic Couplings: The Sacred and the Sexual in the Works of Isaac Bashevis Singer," forthcoming in my collection of *Essays on Singer*.

11. See my *Bibliography of Isaac Bashevis Singer, 1924–1949* (Berne: Peter Lang, 1983), as well as my *Bibliography of Isaac Bashevis Singer, January 1950–June 1952*, Working Papers in Yiddish and East European Jewish Studies, 34 (New York: YIVO Institute for Jewish Research, 1979).

12. Irving Buchen, pp. x–xi et passim; Irving Malin, p. 2.

13. Edward Alexander, p. [9].

14. On the latter, see Mas'ud Zavarzadeh, *The Mythopoeic Reality: The Postwar American Nonfiction Novel* (Urbana: Univ. of Illinois Press, 1976).

15. Anon., *Dos mayse-bukh* (1602; rpt. Buenos Aires: YIVO, 1969); tr. by Joachim Neugroschel as "The Rabbi Who Was Turned into a Werewolf," in *Yenne Velt: The Great Works of Jewish Fantasy and Occult* (1976; rpt. New York: Pocket Books, 1978), pp. 31–43.

16. Alfred Kazin, "Isaac Bashevis Singer and the Mind of God," forthcoming in *Essays on Singer*; Murray Baumgarten: *City Scriptures: Mogern Jewish Writing* (Cambridge, MA: Harvard Univ. Press, 1972).

17. Chone Shmeruk, presentation at the Max Weinreich Center for Advanced Jewish Studies of the YIVO Institute for Jewish Research, 18 Sept. 1978.

18. Susan A. Slotnick, "Isaac Bashevis Singer and the Yiddish Family Saga"; Seth L. Wolitz, "The Two 'Yordim': I. B. Singer's Debt to Dovid Bergelson"; both forthcoming in *Essays on Singer.*

19. Anita Susan Grossman, "Lost in America," *Twentieth Century Literature* [forthcoming].

Chapter 1

1. Harold Bloom, "The Breaking of Form," in *Deconstruction and Criticism,* ed. Harold Bloom et al. *(New York: Seabury, 1979), p. 3.*

2. Bloom, pp. 3–4.

3. Singer's attitude toward the Yiddish literary tradition is complex and not without its contradictions. One the one hand, he claims — expecially in his English-language interviews – to stand almost entirely outside of it. See, for example, his interview with Joel Blocker and Richard Elman, where he states, "I feel myself naturally a part of the Jewish tradition. Very much so! But I wouldn't say I feel myself a part of the Yiddish tradtion" ("An Interview with Isaac Bashevis Singer," in *Critical Views of Isaac Bashevis Singer,* ed. Irving Malin [New York Univ. Press, 1969], p. 9.) On the other hand, he is quick enough to defend the tradition from its detractors, especially when his own relation to that tradition is not at issue. "I don't know what is so parochial," he tells Sanford Pinsker, "so special about Yiddish literature; . . . and if it is bad, I don't care about it at all. Sholom Aleichem would have been a good writer in any language and in any culture"; "Isaac Bashevis Singer: An Interview," *Critique: Studies in Modern Fiction,* 11, No. 2 (1969), 26–39. The issue would merit a detailed investigation.

4. Isaac Bashevis Singer, "Figurn un epizodn fun literarishn fareyn: Der ershter bazukh" [Figures and Episodes from the Writers' Union: The First Visit], *Forverts*, 28 June 1979, p. 3.

5. Two studies of Singer's recasting of inherited conventions are forthcoming in my collection of *Essays on Singer*, viz., Susan A. Slotnick, "Isaac Bashevis Singer and the Yiddish Family Saga"; and Seth L. Wolitz, "The Two 'Yordim': I. B. Singer's Debt to Dovid Bergelson."

6. Dan Miron, *Sholem Aleykehm: Person, Persona, Presence* (New York: YIVO Institute for Jewish Research, 1972); see also Miron's *A Traveler Disguised: A Study in the Rise of Modern Yiddish Fiction in the Nineteenth Century* (New York: Schocken, 1973), pp. 17–33 et passim.

7. "The Jewish Press in Poland, 1938–1939," in Lucjan Dobroszycki and Barbara Kirschenblatt-Gimblett, *Image Before My Eyes: A Photographic History of Jewish Life in Poland, 1964–1939* (New York: Schocken, 1977), p. [263] (Table Six). Yisroel Shayn, surveying Jewish publications in interbellum Poland, located no fewer than 1010 titles – most of them in Yiddish; see his "Materyaln tsu a biblyografye fun yidisher peryodike in Poyln, 1918–1939" [Materials for a Bibliography of Jewish Periodicals in Poland, 1918–1939], in *Studies on Polish Jewry, 1919–1939: The Interplay of Social, Economic and Political Factors on the Struggle of a Minority for Its Existence*, ed. Joshua A. Fishman (New York: YIVO, 1974), pp. 422–500. See also the important volume of memoirs and documentation edited by Yankev Pat, *Fun noentn over* [From the Recent Past], II (Yidish prese in Varshe [The Yiddish Press in Warsaw]; New York: Alveltlekher yidisher kultur-kongres, 1956).

8. The earliest first-person narrative I have located is Singer's "Zaydlus der ershter: Fun a serye dertseylungen 'Dos gedenkbukh fun yeytser-hore" [Zaydlus the First: From the Series of "Devil's Memoirs"], *Svive* [OS], No. 1 (Jan.–Feb. 1943), pp. 11–24; signed Yitskhok Bashevis. It was translated as "Zeidlus the Pope" by Joel Blocker and Elizabeth Pollet in *Short Friday and Other Stories* (New York: Farrar, Straus, 1964), pp. [176–89. Chone Shmeruk cites a letter to him of 10 Aug. 1973 in which Singer confirms that, "oyf vi vayt mayn zikorn dint" [if memory serves], he began to write in the first person only after his arrival in New York; see "The Use of Monologue as a Narrative Technique in the Stories of Isaac Bashevis Singer," in *Der Shpigl un andere dertseylungen* [The Mirror and Other Stories], ed. Chone Shmeruk ([Tel Aviv]: Hebreisher universitet in Yerusholayim, yidish-opteylung; Komitet far yidisher kultur in Yisroel, 1975), p. XIV, n. 18.

9. Irving Howe, *World of Our Fathers* (New York: Harcourt, Brace, 1976), pp. 426–27.

10. E. M. Forster, *Aspects of the Novel* (1927; rpt. New York: Harcourt, Brace, 1954), pp. 25–42, 83–103.

11. Avrom Reyzen, "Di oreme kehile" [The Poor (Jewish) Community], in *Ale verk* [Complete Works], VIII (Oreme gemeynden [Poor Communities]), [7]–14.

12. Isaac Bashevis Singer, "Eyniklekh" [Grandchildren], in *Varshever shriftn* (Warsaw: Literatn-klub baym fareyn fun yidishe literatn un zhurnalistn in Varshe, 1926–27), fourth sequence, pp. 2–11.

13. In *A Young Man in Search of Love*(Garden City, NY: Doubleday, 1978), p. 108, Singer writes, "I liked much better [than *The Magic Mountain* and *Jean Christophe*] Thomas Mann's *The Buddenbrooks. . . ."

14. "Eyniklekh," p. 2.

15. "Eyniklekh," p. 10.

16. Isaac Bashevis Singer, "Tsurikvegs" [The Way Back], *Literarishe bleter*, 5, No. 47 (23 Nov. 1228), 927.

17. For an inventory of Singer's generic tags, see my *Bibliography of Isaac Bashevis Singer, 1924*-1949 (Berne: Peter Lang, 1983).

18. Bogdan Daleszak posits a number of generic constants not dissimilar to my own in his survey of Polish-language *reportazhn* ("An Attempted Theory of the Reportage," *Zagadnienia Rodzajów Literackich*, 8, No. 1 (1965), [52]–73. Daleszak's otherwise acute analysis is weakened by a preoccupation with the literal historicity of the *reportazhn* he discusses, rather than with their status as narrative acts or artifacts.

19. Though offered several opportunities to leave Warsaw for America, Opotshinski was resolutely to refuse and, after the occupation of Poland, continued to write *reportazhn* in the Warsaw Ghetto; these were collected and published by Ber Mark as *Reportazhn fun varshever geto* [*Reportazhn* from the Warsaw Ghetto] (Warsaw: Yidbukh, 1954). For further information, see Rine Oper, "Mayn bruder Perets Opotshinski" [My Brother Perets Opotshinski], in Perets Opotshinski, *Gezamlte shriftn* [Collected Writings] (New York: privately published, 1951), pp. 5–60.

20. Perets Opotshinski, "In Krashinskis gortn" [In Kraszinski Gardens], in *Gezamlte shriftn*, pp. 154–60; further references have been incorporated into the text.

21. Isaac Bashevis Singer, "Sale: A bild" [Sale: A Portrait], *Literarishe bleter*, 9, No. 1 (1 Jan. 1932), 7–8.

22. Virginia Woolf, "The Shooting Party," *Harper's Bazaar* (London), March 1938, 72, 100, 102. Rpt. (rev.) in *A Haunted House* (1944; rpt. London: Hogarth, 1967), pp. 59–68.

23. Ring Lardner, *"Clemo Uti* (The Water Lillies)," in *The Ring Lardner Reader*, ed. Maxwell Geismar (New York: Scribner's, 1963), pp. 599–601.

24. Isaac Bashevis Singer, "A zokn: A khronik" [An Old Man: A Chronicle], *Globus: Khoydesh-zhurnal far literatur*, [1], No. 3 (Sept. 1932), 39–49; signed Yitskhok Bashevis. Further references to "A zokn" in the original Yiddish have been incorporated into the text after the letter *Y.* Trans. as "The Old Man" by Norbert Guterman and Elaine Gottlieb, in *Gimpel the Fool and Other Stories* (New York: Noonday, 1959), pp. 1479; further references have been incorporated into the text after the letter *E*.

25. Isaac Bashevis Singer, "Acknowledgements," in *Gimpel the Fool*, n. pag.; Singer errs in the date of publication.

26. See David Neal Miller, " 'Don't Force Me to Tell You the Ending': Closure in the Short Fiction of Sh. Rabinovitsh (Sholem Aleykhem)," *Neophilologus*, 66, 1 (Jan. 1982), 102–10.

27. In contrast to the *reportazhn* and minimalist fictions, Singer's more conventional short fiction appeared without generic tagging, or with generic designations clearly attributable to an editor's hand. Thus, for example, "Der yid fun Bovl" [The Jew from Babylon] was originally published without generic tag in a journal of which Singer was co-editor (*Globus*, [1], No. 2 [July (i.e. Aug.) 1932], 17–27. When reprinted in a later collection edited by others, however, it bore the added subtitle *dertseylung* [short story] (*Antologye fun der yidisher proze in Poyln tsvishn beyde velt-milkhomes, 1914*–1939 [Anthology of Yiddish Prose in Interbellum Poland, 1914–1939], ed. Y.-Y. Trunk and Arn Tseytlin [New York: Tsiko, 1946], pp. 43–52).

28. There is even a suggestion, not further elaborated upon, that the old man had died and was leaving the apartment by hearse – and that, accordingly, the rest of "A zokn" might best be considered as fantasy or dream vision. As I discuss in chapter four, the juxtaposition of fantastic and quotidien elements in a single story was later to become Singer's primary mode of generic mixing.

29. On Benjamin of Tudela, see C[ecil] R[oth]'s short article in the *Encyclopedia Judaica*, IV (Jerusalem: Keter, 1972), cols. 535–38. The critical edition is by Marcus Nathan Adler, *The Itinerary of Benjamin of Tudela* (London, 1907; rpt. New York: Feldheim, n.d.).

30. The most accessible edition is that edited by Ilse-Marie Barth, Universal-Bibliothek Nr. 4343/a/b (Stuttgart: Philipp Reclam, 1964). Of the nearly-identical critical editions published in the Neudrucke dt. Literaturwerke des XVI. und XVII. Jahrhunderts, the East German edn. is preferable: in it, the texts of both "first" editions of the first part are printed on facing pages (*Schelmuffsky,* 2nd [rev.] edn., ed. Wolfgang Hecht [Halle/Salle: Max Niemeyer, 1956]).

31. Nonfictional pieces follow the same pattern: eleven of the twenty-four nonfictional columns published between 1925 and 1933 are of the "A shmues mit . . ." [A Conversation with . . .] variety; seven others are reviews of recently-published books.

32. Cf. n. 27, supra.

33. Isaac Bashevis Singer, "Oyfn oylem-hatoye" [In the World of Chaos], *Di yidishe velt: Khoydesh-shrift far literatur, kritik, kunst un kultur,* No. 1 (April 1928), pp. 53–64; signed Yitskhok Bashevis. Singer mentions this story, which has not been reprinted, in *A Young Man in Search of Love* (Garden City, N. Y.: Doubleday, 1978), pp. 132–33.

34. Isaac Bashevis Singer, *Der sotn in Goray: A mayse fun fartsaytns* [Satan in Goray: A Tale of Bygone Days] (1933; collected Warsaw: Biblyotek fun yidishn p.e.n.–klub, 1935; rpt. (rev.) New York: Farlag Matones, 1943; rpt. Jerusalem: Hebreisher universitet, 1972); tr. as *Satan in Goray* by Jacob Sloan (New York: Noonday, 1955). A sound interpretive close reading of *Der sotn in Goray* is still lacking; there is, however, an excellent discussion of Singer's use of language in the novel by Chone Shmeruk, in *Der shpigl,* pp. vii–xi.

35. Alfred Kazin identifies parallels between Hawthorne's fundamental attitudes and Singer's, without, however, discussing similarities in their works; see "Isaac Bashevis Singer and the Mind of God" in my forthcoming collection of *Essays on Singer.* On Hawthorne's attempt to reconcile fictive and everyday elements in his fiction, see Mary Rohrberger's excellent chapter on "Howthorne's Literary Theory and Its Relation to His Short Stories" in her *Hawthorne and the Modern Short Story* (The Hague: Mouton, 1966), pp. [16]–24.

36. Nathaniel Hawthorne, Preface to *The House of the Seven Gables: A Romance* (Boston: Ticknor, Reed & Fields, 1851), n. pag. I am grateful to A. S. Grossman for having brought Hawthorne's prefaces to my attention in this context.

37. Nathaniel Hawthorne, Preface to *The Blithedale Romance* (Boston: Ticknor, Reed & Fields, 1952), pp. iii–iv.

38. Nathaniel Hawthorne, Preface [15 Dec. 1859] to *The Marble Faun; or, the Romance of Monte Beni* (Boston: Ticknor and Fields, 1860), I, vii. Hawthorne writes that "no author, without a trial, can conceive of the difficulty of writing a romance about a country where there is no shadow of antiquity . . . nor anything but a commonplace prosperity, in broad and simple daylight, as is happily the case with my dear native land. It will be very long . . . before romance-writers may find congenial and easily handled themes, either in the annals of our stalwart republic, or in any characteristic and probable events in our individual lives."

39. On the historical novel, see Murray Baumgarten, "The Historical Novel: Some Postulates," *Clio*, 4, No. 2 (Feb. 1975), 173–82.

40. See "'Don't Force Me to Tell You the Ending,'" p. 105.

41. Nokhem-Meyer Shaykevitsh (pseud. Shomer), *Der Baron un di markize: A hekhst-interesanter roman* [The Baron and the Marchioness: A Highly Interesting Novel] (Odessa: Bletnitski, 1902).

42. A.-M. D. (=Azik-Meyer Dik?), *Malke veHadase* (etc.) [Malke and Hadassah (etc.)] (Vilna: N.p., 1887).

43. Nokhem-Meyer shaykevitsh (pseud. Shomer), *Di geheyme yidn: A roman fun der yidisher geshikhte in Shpanyen* [The Secret Jews: A Novel About Jewish history in Spain] (New York: Hebrew Publishing Co., n.d.).

44. There has not, to the best of my knowledge, been a serious discussion of the conventional historical novel in Yiddish. By contrast, the Yiddish *roman-fleuve* has had more than its share of critical attention, most likely because of the greater prestige the genre enjoys. See, for example, Susan A. Slotnock, "*Di familye Mushkat* and the Tradition of the Yiddish Family Saga," in my forthcoming collection of *Essays on Singer.*

45. Isaac Bashevis Singer, *Der zindiker meshiekh: Historisher roman* [The Sinning Messiah: An Historical Novel], *Forverts*, 5 Oct. 1935. p. 12.

46. Ab. Kan (Abraham Cahan), "Yankev Frank: Der firer fun der yidisher sekte (etc.)" [Yankev Frank: The Leader of the Jewish Sect (etc.)], *Forverts*, 5 Oct. 1935, p. 12

47. Kan was, of course, himself the author of a "realistish-historisher roman." On Kan as author, see Jules Chametzky, *From the Ghetto: The Fiction of Abraham Cahan* (Amherst: Univ. of Massachusetts Press, 1972).

48. Amado Alonso, *Ensayo sobre la novela historica* (Buenos Aires, 1942), pp. 86–87; cited by Baumgarten, p. 177.

49. Murray Baumgarten, p. 177.

50. In his recently-published volume of near-autobiography, *Lost in America* (Garden City, N.Y.: Doubleday, 1981), Singer mentions a novel which, in context, can only be *Der zindiker meshiekh*. Curiously, he seems uncomfortable – in retrospect, at least – with narrative prerogatives substantially less radical than those I discuss in this chapter: "I had always had an aversion for digressions and flashbacks but I now resorted to them, amazed what I was doing" (p. 139).

51. These conventions are catalogued by Georg Lukács in *The Historical Novel* (1937), tr. Hannah and Stanley Mitchell (London: Merlin, 1962), esp. in his section of "The Classical Form of the Historical Novel," pp. 19–88.

52. Alexander Welsh, "Contrast of Styles in the Waverly Novels," *Novel*, 6 (Spring 1973), 228.

53. Isaac Bashevis Singer, *Der zindiker meshiekh*, *Forverts*, 8 Oct. 1935, p. 7.

54. Murray Baumgarten, pp. 177–78.

55. Isaac Bashevis Singer, *Der zindiker meshiekh*, *Forverts*, 9 Oct. 1935, p. 9.

56. Isaac Bashevis Singer, "Author's Note," in *My Father's Court* (New York: Farrar, Straus, 1966), p. vii; the note is not present in the Yiddish edition.

57. Though I have discussed Singer's recasting of inherited genres in this chapter, his recasting of specific works from the canon has not yet received the critical attention it merits. The article by Seth L. Wolitz on "The Two 'Yordim': Isaac Bashevis Singer Confronts Dovid Bergelson," forthcoming in my collection of *Essays on Singer*, is the first of what should prove to be a fertile area of research. One of the more striking of Singer's counterpieces is his "Der kurtser Fraytik" [Short Friday], *Di tsukunft*, 50, No. 1 (Jan. 1945), 19–23; tr. as "Short Friday" by Joseph Singer and Roger Klein, in *Short Friday and Other Stories* (New York: Farrar, Straus, 1964), pp. [229]–43. "Der kurtser fraytik" both invokes and parodies one of Lamed Shapiro's better-known stories, "Der rov un di rebetsin" [The Rabbi and the Rabbi's Wife], in *Di yidishe melukhe un andere zakhn* [The Jewish Government and Other Things] (New York: Yidish leben, 1929), pp. [283]–85; tr. as "The Rabbi and the Rebbetsin," in *The Jewish Government and Other Stories*, ed. and tr. Curt Leviant (New York: Twayne, 1971), pp. 51–53.

58. In his introduction to Singer's *Der shpigl un andere dertseylungen* [The Mirror and Other Stories], p. xvii, n. 25, Shmeruk points out that Singer's use of barnyard fowl as first-person narrators recalls Sholom Aleichem's earlier use of the identical narrative situation: Sholem Rabinovitsh (pseud. Sholom Aleichem), "Dos porfolk" [The Couple] (1909), in *Ale verk* [Complete Works], VIII (Mayses far yidishe kinder [Tales for Jewish Children], 1), [127]–53; tr. as "The Pair" by Irving Howe and Eliezer Greenberg (1954; rpt. New York: Shocken, 1973), pp. 192–205; "Kapores" [Scapegoats] (1903), in *Ale verk*, VIII, [113]–26; cf. Isaac Bashevis Singer, "Kukuriku" [Cockadoodledoo] by Ruth Whitmen, in *The Seance and Other Stories* (New York: Farrar, Straus, 1968), pp. 89–94. Although Shmeruk astutely notes the parallels in narrative situation, he apparently failed to recognize Singer's aggressively parodic intent.

Chapter 2

1. The first hiatus in Singer's productive career extended from October 1933 through mid-1935.

2. Singer has been a consistent opponent of both politically engaged writing and the avant-garde; often he (incorrectly) equates the two. See for example, "Tsu der frage fun dikhtung un politik" [Poetry and Politics], *Globus*, [1], No. 3 (Sept. 1932), 39–49; signed Yitskhok Bashevis.

3. Chapter Four contains a discussion of this wholly imaginary hiatus.

4. Singer ceased publishing after the appearance of "In a leydiker shtub: Dertseylung" [In an Empty Home: A Story], *Forverts*, 11 April 1937, p. 3; signed Yitskhok Bashevis. His next appearance in print was not until twenty-four months later.

5. Nor, at this stage in his career, could there have been any literarily exploitable discrepancy between Bashevis-Singer's public persona and the facts of his private life independently known to his readers: neither the one nor the other had yet attracted much attention. In contrast to Rabinovitsh and Clemens, then, the locus of Singer's early persona-building was wholly textual.

6. Isaac Bashevis Singer, in *My Father's Court* (New York: Farrar, Straus and Giroux, 1966), p. vii. The note is not present in the Yiddish edition, *Mayn tatns bezdn-shtub* (New York: Kval, 1956), where it would have been superfluous: Yiddish readers already knew the name under which Singer had earlier published these pieces in the *Forverts*.

7. Joel Blocker and Richard Elman, "An Interview with Isaac Bashevis Singer," In *Critical Views of Isaac Bashevis Singer*, ed. Irving Malin (New York: New York University Press, 1969), p. 8.

8. Marshall Breger and Bob Barnhart, "A Conversation with Isaac Bashevis Singer," in *Critical Views*, pp. 32–33.

9. Chone Shmeruk, "The Use of Monologue as a Narrative Technique in the Stories of Isaac Bashevis Singer," in *Der shpigl un andere dertseylungen* [The Mirror and Other Stories], ed. Chone Shmeruk ([Tel Aviv]: Hebreisher universitet in Yerusholayim, Yidish-opteylung; Komitet far yidisher kultur in Yisroel, 1975), pp. xxiv–xxv; my translation.

10. A discussion of this unremarkable novel would not contribute substantially to my investigation. "Di familye Mushkat: Roman [The Family Mushkat: A Novel] commenced publication in the *Forverts* on 17 Nov. 1945 and concluded on 1 May 1948. For a complete citation, see my *Bibliography of Isaac Bashevis Singer, 1924–1949*, at B539, B554, B662, and B750.

11. Isaac Bashevis Singer, "A yidisher shrayber makht an onklage kegn a yidishn farlag" [A Yiddish Writer Registers a Complaint Against a Yiddish Publisher], *Forverts*, 24 Sept. 1946, p. 5; signed Yitskhok Varshavski.

12. Isaac Bashevis Singer, "An interesante debate: Hot Hitler vild gemakht Daytshland oder der 'daytsher gayst' hot geshafn Hitlern?" [An Interesting Controversy: Did Hitler Uncivilize German or Did the German Spirit Create Hitler?], *Forverts*, 10 Jan. 1943, p. 3; "Der heldisher kamf fun yidn kegn di natsis in der varshever geto" [Heroic Battle of Jews Against Nazis in the Warsaw Ghetto], *Forverts*, 4 July 1943, pp. 2, 4; "Di yidishe shprakh un kultur lebt iber ir greste krizis" [Yiddish Language and Culture Undergo Their Greatest Crisis], *Forverts*, 4 Dec. 1944, pp. 4, 3; "Stsenes fun yomerlekhn dales in Varshe" [Scenes of Bitter Poverty in Warsaw], *Forverts*, 6 Aug. 1944, sec. 2, p. 3; "Hitlers geshray az er firt milkhomes kegn yidn" [Hitler's Battle Cry Against the Jews], *Forverts*, 7 Aug. 1944, pp. 2, 3; all signed Yitskhok Varshavski.

13. Marshall Breger and Bob Barnhart, "A Conversation with Isaac Bashevis Singer," p. 33.

14. This, at least, was the case until well into the 1950's, when Varshavski was to begin his series of personal memoirs. But by then there no longer was a pseudonymous persona to protect: Singer, Varshavski, and Bashevis had, effectively, merged identities and narrative strategies.

15. Thus discussions centering on the nature of Singer's political views – such as Edward Alexander's disappointing book on *Isaac Bashevis Singer* in the Twayne World Authors Series (Boston: Twayne, 1980) miss the point: Singer is less a political conservative than a self-assertively apolitical writer; his works do not, except in the limited sense that I develop in this chapter, invite or reward examination in light of their socio-political content. Cf. Singer's "Ven shrayber vern politiker vos vert fun der literatur" [What Happens to Literature When Writers Turn Politicians], *Forverts*, 27 March 1944, pp. 2, 3; signed Yitskhok Varshavski.

16. Isaac Bashevis Singer, "The Yearning Heifer," in *Passions and Other Stories* (New York: Farrar, Straus, and Giroux, 1975), p. 96.

17. Singer published a number of book reviews in *Di tsukunft"* (New York) in 1939 and 1940 under the general rubric "Fun der bikhervelt." [The World of Books]; these were his only works of this period signed Bashevis. Singer typically addressed himself to prose works by worthy writers of realistic or naturalistic bent, respected abroad though all but unknown to American readers – Mikhl Burshtin (Poland), Pinkhes Goldhar (Australia), Sh. Izban (Palestine), among others.

18. Isaac Bashevis Singer, "A litvisher yid, velkher iz geven a betler, a kemfer far emes un eyner fun di greste filozofn in der velt" [A Lithuanian Jew Who Was a Beggar, Fighter for the Truth, and One of the World's Great Philosophers], *Forverts*, 16 April 1939, sec. 2, p. 3; 23 April 1939, sec. 2, p. 3; signed Yitshkhok Varshavski.

19. Isaac Bashevis Singer, "A yidisher diktator in Drohobitsh, mit velkher s'hot gekokht gants Galitsye" [The Jewish Dictator of Drohobycz – The Rage of Galicia], *Forverts*, 30 April 1939, p. 7; 7 May 1939, p. 5; signed Yitskhok Varshavski.

20. Jonathan Culler, *Structuralist Poetics: Structuralism, Linguistics, and the Study of Lieterature* (Ithaca, N.Y.: Cornell University Press, 1975), p. 138.

21. It is important to distinguish between *reportazh* – a literary genre – and reportage (= reportorial nonfiction). If Singer often blurs generic distinctions in specific works, the general distinction is clear enough.

22. It is interesting, if not particularly germane to my discussion, to note the absence of disparaging commentary on Gentile customs or behavior in "A yidisher diktator." Though Jews do differ from non-Jews – in, above all, their attitude toward the death penalty – Varshavski

declines to depict the Catholic clergy as having seduced or coerced Zalmen into conversion, nor does he mention the pogroms which might have been expected to follow Zalmen's overthrow. This atypically (perhaps ahistorically) benign depiction of Jewish-Gentile relations continues to the present day; anti-Semitic tendencies among the Polish peasantry are depicted as ethnographically noteworthy, rather than threatening. See, for example, "A Tutor in the Village," in *Passions*, pp. 148–61.

23. This is what I take to be the central thematic concern of *Der kuntsnmakher fun Lublin* (1958; coll. tel Aviv: Y.-L. Perets, 1971); tr. by Elaine Gottlieb and Joseph Singer as *The Magician of Lublin* (New York: Noonday, 1960).

24. On the admissability of *daytshmerizmen* in standard Yiddish, see Maks Vaynraykh's classic polemic, "Daytshmerish toyg nit" [Daytshmerish Is Wrong], *Yidish far ale* (Vilna) 1 (1938), 97–106. That Vaynraykh's concern was not exaggerated is persuasively documented by Mordkhe Schaechter in "The 'Hidden Standard': A Study of Competing Influences in Standardization," in *The Field of Yiddish: Studies in Language, Folklore, and Literature*, III (The Hague: Mouton, 1969), 284–304.

25. Uriel Weinreich, *Modern English-Yiddish Yiddish-English Dictionary* (New York: McGraw-Hill, 1968), p. 667.

26. Nokhem Stutshkov (Stutchkoff), *Der oytser fun der yidisher shprakh* (New York: YIVO, 1950), sex. 366, p. 344; sec. 381, p. 368. Maks Vaynraykh was Stutshkov's editor and stylistic arbiter.

27. Stutshkov, sex. 381, p. 368, records the following compounds with *mayse*: *folks-mayse* [folk tale], *shabes-mayse* [Sabbath tale], *tsoyber-mayse* [supernatural tale], *lign-mayse* [tall tale], *avantur-mayse* [adventure tale], *bove-mayse* [tale from the *Bovebukh*], *bobe-mayse* [old wives' tale], *mayse nisim* [miracle tale], *mayse-bukh* [collection of tales; *Mayse-bukh*], *mayse-shehoye* [true story].

28. In a public discussion of his works at the State University of New York at Albany on 2 Oct. 1980, Singer began by dismissing his journalistic writings. When, however, I dissented by praising them and discussing several texts, Singer admitted to tentative plans of publishing a culling of his *Daily Jottings*—the proposed volume's working title.

29. From 1943 through 1945, Singer also published a total of five short stories signed Yitskhok Bashevis. They were: "Zaydlus der ershter: Fun a serye dertseylunger 'Dos gedenkbukh fun yeytser-hore" [Zaydlus

the First: From the Series of "Devil's Memoirs"], *Svive*, [OS], No. 1 (Jan.-Feb. 1943, pp. 11–24; tr. as "Zeidlus the Pope" by Joel Blocker and Elizabeth Pollet in *Short Friday and Other Stories* (New York: Farrar, Straus and Giroux, 1964), pp. [176]–89; "Der roye veeyne-nire: Fun der serye dertseylungen 'Dos gedenkbukh fun yeytser-hore'" [Seer but Not Seen: From the Series of "Devil's Memoirs"], *Svive* [OS], No. 4 (July–Aug. 1943), pp. 16–31; tr. by Norbert Guterman and Elaine Gottlieb as "The Unseen" in *Gimpel the Fool and Other Stories* (New York: Noonday, *Tsukunft*, 50, No. 1 (Jan. 1945), 19–23; tr. by Joseph Singer and Roger Klein in *Short Friday and Other Stories*, pp. 228–43; "Gimpl tam" [Gimpl the Fool], *Yidisher kemfer*, 24, Whole no. 593 (30 Mar. 1945), 17–20; tr. by Saul Bellow in *Gimpel the Fool and Other Stories*, pp. 3–21; "Der katlen" [The Wife Killer], *Yidisher kemfer*, 25, Whole no. 615 (7 Sept. 1945), 52–56; tr. by Shlomo Katz as "The Wife Killer: A Folk Tale" in *Gimpel the Fool and Other Stories*, pp. 77–88.

30. The "medical data" is impressive: Singer averaged about four published pieces a year between 1924 and 1933, seventy-seven between 1939 and 1948; the latter is, certainly, a healthier figure.

31. Examples are, respectively, "Babske refues inem yidishn lebn fun amol" [Old Wives' Cures Among Jews of Yesterday], *Forverts*, 12 July 1942, sec. 2, p. 2; "A naye grupe in der yidisher literatur?" [A New Yiddish Literary Group?], *Forverts*, 26 Dec. 1948, sec. 2, p. 5; "Romanen un libes bay khayes, beheymes un feygl" [Love and Romance Among Birds and Beasts], *Forverts*, 19 May 1940, sex. 2, pp. 2, 4; "Mames, shvigers, shvester un brider, vos makhn a beyz lebn tsvishn man un vayb" [Mothers, Mothers-in-Law, Sisters and Brothers Who Promote Trouble Between Husband and Wife], 14 April 1940, sec. 2, pp. 2, 4; all signed Yitskhok Varshavski.

32. Both concepts are subsumed by the English term *moral*; strictly speaking, the *muser-haskl* is the moral proper, the *nimshl* a transition from text to *muser-haskl* making explicit the allusive equation (e.g., the fox equals an unscrupulously acquisitive person). See Barbara Kirshenblatt-Gimblett, "The Concept and Varieties of Narrative Performance in East European Jewish Culture," in *Explorations in the Ethnography of Speaking*, ed. Richard Bauman and Jeol Sherzer (Cambridge, England: Cambridge Univ. Press, 1974), pp. 302–06 et passim.

33. Singer distinguishes between his years as a stringer and those as a staff writer for the *Forverts*. This distinction, at the *Forverts* at least, has always been a fine one: staff writers, like regular stringers, are expected to produce an individually-negotiated amount of copy for an individually-negotiated salary. Whatever effect Singer's change of

employment status might have had on his personal affairs, it was in no way reflected in the quantity or quality of his writings.

34. The genesis and private meaning of D. Segal is similarly opaque. *Bashevis* recalls Singer's mother, *Varshavski* the city of his early adulthood. What *Segal* recalls only Singer could tell us.

35. L[eonard] P[rager], "Isaac Bashevis Singer," in *Encyclopedia Judaica*, IVB (Jerusalem: Keter, 1972), col. 294.

36. In fairness, two of the latter were novels: *Di familye Muskhat* (*The Family Moskat*), see n. 10; "Der feter fun Amerike: Roman" [The Uncle from America: A Novel], *Forverts*, 17 Dec. 1949 through 3 March 1951.

37. Segal's inevitable absence from all public functions – as well as from the editorial offices at which he purportedly labored – could not long have escaped notice. Moreover, there was a certain laxity in the bylining of Segal's articles: "Nekhayme Vinavers muzikalish verk 'Der zibeter tog' " [Nekhayme Vinaver's *The Seventh Day*], *Forverts*, 13 Dec. 1946, p. 6, was attributed to *B*. Segal, and "Yidn vos zaynen avek fun der heym un gelozt zukhn glik" [Jews Who Made Off to Seek Their Fortune], *Forverts*, 8 April 1947, pp. 2, 6, to *A*. Segal; in neither case was a correction printed.

38. The Yiddish literary world is one of the open secret. Few Yiddish literati, for example, do not know or could not ascertain the identity of A. Forsher (i.e. Yosl and Khane Mlotek), author of the popular and well-written weekend series, "Perl fun der yidisher poezye" [Pearls of Yiddish Poetry], or that of the current respondent to "Bintl Briv" inquiries. D. Segal seems, on the other hand, to have been a mystery even to those otherwise literarily *au courant*. Though I have already acknowledged his assistance in the preface, I would like again to express my gratitude to Dr. Elias Schulman, a scholar of encyclopedic erudition, for having, as it were, spilled the scholarly beans on Segal's extra-literary identity several years prior to the publication of Prager's article.

39. Isaac Bashevis Singer, "Geburt-kontrol – A frage nit bloyz farn privatn lebn nor oykh far der politik fun felker un regirungen" [Birth Control: More than a Privat Matter – One That Touches the Politics of States and Peoples], *Forverts*, 14 Feb. 1943, p. 3; signed Yitskhok Varshavski.

40. Isaac Bashevis Singer, "Mener vos vern oyf di eltere yorn romantish" [Man Who Turns Romantic in Old Age], *Forverts*, 6 Oct. 1944, pp. 2, 6; signed D. Segal. *Romantish*, in this context, has an explicitly sexual denotation.

41. The first of these appeals was "Mir viln nemen undezere lezer far shutfim" [We Want Our Readers as Partners], *Forverts*, 24 Sept. 1945, p. 2; it was followed shortly by "Fragn tsu undzere lezer vegn purim un peysekh" [we Ask Our Readers about Purim and Passover], *Forverts*, 13 Feb. 1946, p. 2; both signed Yitskhok Varshavski.

42. Replies to "Mir viln nemen undzere lezer far shutfim" provided grist for no fewer than five columns of culled responses, "Fragn tsu undzere lezer . . ." for an additional five. One suspects that the printed replies are an admixture of genuine responses and author-written ringers.

43. An unguarded reference to an historical person by her real name in one of the later memoirs actually led to an unpleasant scene between the woman's son and Isaac Singer at the editorial offices of the *Forverts*.

44. Isaac Bashevis Singer, "Er hot a milyon dolar, ober er veyst nit vos m'tut mit zey" [He Has a Million Dollars He Doesn't Know What to Do With]. *Forverts*, 7 Feb. 1947, p. 5; signed D. Segal.

45. There are echoes of this situation in one of singer's recent fictions: "Sam Palka and David Vishkover," in *Passions and Other Stories* (New York: Farrar, Straus and Giroux, 1975), pp. 133–47.

46. Isaac Bashevis Singer, "Lezer fun *Forverts* gibn eytses a yidn vegn vi oystsugebn a milyon dolar" [*Forward* Readers Advise How to Spend a Million Dollars], *Forverts*, 17 Feb. 1947, p. 5; signed D. Segal.

47. Segal would continue to solicit reader replies to relatively innocuous questions, some of them not even motivated by an initial incident or report; as late as 1950, he was asking his readers to send in accounts of "Di greste iberrashung in mayn lebn" [The Greatest Surprise in My Life].

48. Meyer Peskof, "Der militerishe shnayder Bornshteyn, velkher hot geshikt zayne finf zin in milkhome" [Bornstein, Tailor to the Military, Who Sent His Five Sons to War], *Forverts*, 21 March 1946, p. 5.

49. "Nayes fun yidishn lebn in Palestine: Sovet-rusland vet zikh nit mishn in der frage fun emigratsye keyn Erets-yisroel" [News of Jewish Life in Palestine: Soviet Russia Won't Interfere with Jewish Emigration to Palestine], *Forverts*, 26 Jan. 1945, p. 5; unsigned.

50. Isaac Bashevis Singer, "Er hot zikh getrofn mit zayn 'geshtorbener' gelibter" [He Met His "Dead" Lover], *Forverts*, 21 March 1946, p. 5; signed D. Segal.

51. In its entirety, the subtitle reads: "Er hot gegloybt, az zi iz umgekumen durkh di natsis, ober er hot zi begegnt in gas. —A tsuzamentref fun tsvey 'meysim'. —A drame, vos iz oft nit dramatish. —Di psikhologishe shverikaytn zikh tsutsupasn tsu der virklekhayt. —Yesurim endern mentshn nit azoy fil vi men gleybt" [He Thought the Nazis Had Killed Her but He Met Her in the Street; A Meeting of Two "Corpses"; A Drama Which Often Isn't Dramatic; The Psychological Difficulties of Adjusting to Reality; Suffering Does Not Change People as Much as One Might Think].

52. Isaac Bashevis Singer, "Er gloybt in zahn vayb khotsh ale faktn zaynen kegn ir" [Believes in His Wife Even Though Facts are Stacked Against Her], *Forverts*, 19 Jan. 1945, p. 5; signed D. Segal.

53. Isaac Bashevis Singer, "Di tokhter hot zikh ayngeredt az zi iz an aktrise" [Daughter Persuades Herself She's an Actress], *Forverts* 11 May 1945, p. 5; signed D. Segal.

56. Isaac Bashevis Singer, "Ir khosn hot zikh farlibt in ir mame" [Her Fiancé Fell in Love with Her Mother], *Forverts*, 23 March 1945, p. 7; signed D. Segal.

55. Isaac Bashevis singer, "Er hot zikh geget mit zayn froy un zi genumen far a gelibter" [Divorced His Wife and Took Her as Lover", *Forverts*, 21 May 1945, p. 5; signed D. Segal.

56. Isaac Bashevis Singer, "Er hot forgeshtelt zayn gelibte als zayn shvester" [He Introduced His Love as His Sister], *Forverts*, 26 Jan. 1945, P. 5; signed D. Segal.

57. John M. Ellis, *The Theory of Literary Criticism: A Logical Analysis* (Berkeley: Univ. of California Press, 1974), p. 147.

58. See n. 58.

59. This situation obtained at least through 1971, when the failure of the *Forverts'* more traditional competitor, the *Tog-Morgn-zhurnal*, led to a marked slackening of the former's hostility toward matters religious; whether as a sign of softening with age or as purely commercial bid for a broader share of the declining Yiddish readership, the *Forverts* has lately begun to print Sabbath candle-lighting times and even Talmudic commentaries. In 1979, "Arbeter fun ale lender fareynikt zikh" [Workers of the World, Unite] was removed from the masthead.

60. Roman Jakobson, *Novejsaja russkaja poezja* (Prague, 1921); cited by Victor Erlich in his *Russian Formalism: History—Doctrine* (The Hague: Mouton, 1965), pp. 7, 227, et passim.

61. In the surrounding articles, subtitles appear either at the head of the first column or, in the case of the "Bintl briv," directly under the multi-column title.

62. The first of these was "Der shrayberklub" [The Writers' Club], which ran during 1950 and 1951; see my *Bibliography of Isaac Bashevis Singer, January 1950*–June 1952, Working Papers in Yiddish and East European Jewish Studies, 34 (New York: YIVO Institute for Jewish Research, 1979), for details.

63. Isaac Bashevis Singer, "A froy hot fartroyt dem redaktor a vikhtikn sod" [Woman Trusts Editor with Important Secret], *Forverts*, 15 Dec. 1947; signed D. Segal.

64. Isaac Bashevis Singer, "Lezer fun *Forverts* zogn zikh aroys vegn a vikhtiker frage" [*Forward* Readers Speak Out on Crucial Issue], *Forverts*, 22 Dec. 1947, p. 5; signed D. Segal.

65. Isaac Bashevis Singer, "Mir viln nemen undzere lezer far shut-fim" [We Want Our Readers as Partners], see n. 43.

66. Isaac Bashevis Singer, "Vi eltern darfn handlen ven zeyer tokhter firt a libe mit a farheyratn man" [How Parents Should Act When Their Doughter Has an Affair with a Married Man], *Forverts*, 18 Dec. 1947, pp. 2, 7; signed Menakhem Podolyer.

67. "Khotsh di muter hot tsu im a shlekht gefil, hot zi zikh gezegnt mit im mit der meynung, az er iz oyf zayn shteyger a simpatisher mentsh. Er hot di tokhter nisht opgenart" [Although the mother had had ill feelings toward him, she parted from him thinking that he was, after his fashion, a likeable person. He never deceived her daughter], p. 5.

68. Podolyer would have figured in the seventh volume of the *Leksikon fun der nayer yidisher literatur* [Lexicon of Modern Yiddish Literature] (New York: Alveltekher yidisher kultur-kongres, 1968); he is also absent from its predecessor, Zalmen Reyzen's *Leksikon fun der yidisher literatur, prese un filologye* [Lexicon of Yiddish Literature, Press, and Philology], II (Vilna: B. Kletskin, 1927).

69. This was the topic of my presentation at the Second International Conference on Research in Yiddish Language and Literature (Oxford), July 1983.

70. Mordkhe Schaechter points out that, historically, *bikhl* was used to refer to all secular works in book format, regardless of their size, and that the term was unmarked. (*Seyfer* served a parallel function for

religious texts.) See his *Yiddish II* [in press]. And, indeed, the passage by Rabinovitsh cited in n. 72 demonstrates that, in 1888, *bikhl* carried no negative connotation (except, of course, to those who rejected secular literature a priori). But Schaechter overlooks the fact that secular Yiddish – and, for that matter, Hebrew – publications were, at least through the late nineteenth century, almost always in duodecimo or chapbook format; that is, they *were*, literally, *bikhlekh*. See David G. Roskies' important contribution to Yiddish bibliology, "The Medium and Message of the Maskilic Chapbook," *Jewish Social Studies*, 41, Nos. 3–4 (Summer-Fall 1979), 275–90. In 1947, however, the use of *bikhl* by a secular, albeit conservative, journalist could only be disparagingly intended.

71. Sh. Rabinovitsh, *Shomers mishpet* (Berdichev, 1888). Even at his most biting, Rabinovitsh does not accuse Shaykevith of inflicting more than literary damages: "Zet, vi vayt er hot fardorbn dos gefil mitn geshmak funem poshetn lezer az . . . yedes meydl [iz] azoy ongefilt mit Shomers puste, vilde, megushemdike romanen, az [ir] kop iz farshlogn mit fantazyes, az zey kenen shoyn . . . keyn rekht bikhl in der hant nisht nemen . . . [So thoroughly has he corrupted the feelings and tastes of the common reader that every girl is so full of his empty, wild, crude novels (/romances), her head so battered by fantasy, that she no longer can hold a proper book in her hands] (p. 10).

72. A year later Singer would make explicit his changed attitude toward fictiveness in "Emes un sheker in der literatur" [Truth and falsehood in Literature], *Forverts*, 25 Jan. 1948, sec. 2, p. 5; signed Yitskhok Varshavski.

73. See n. 31. *Yeytser-hore* is, more precisely, the evil inclination personified.

Chapter 3

1. Segal was still appearing, albeit with somewhat lesser frequency, in the pages of the *Forverts* as late as 1964 – the last year for which bibliographical information is available.

2. "Vi azoy shvues iz gevorn der yontev fun der toyre" [How Shavuous Became the Holiday of the Torah], for example, is a nearly word-for-word reproduction of Singer's earlier "Shvues – der yontev fun nemen di toyre" [Shavuous – The Holiday of Receiving the Torah]; the former was published in the *Forverts* for 3 June 1949, p. 2, the latter in the *Forverts* for 6 June 1957. "Shteyner vos faln arop fun himl" [Rocks

That Fall from the Skies] was, similarly lightly edited to become "Vos es falt alts arop fun him!" [The Things That Fall from the Sky!]; *Forverts*, 12 Nov. 1944, pp. 4, 3; 14 Feb. 1957, pp. 2, 3, resp. All were signed Yitskhok Varshavski. Many other examples might be cited.

3. By contrast, only two pieces with this title appeared in 1950 – the first year for which it was recorded; see my *Bibliography of Isaac Bashevis Singer,* January 1950–June 1952, Working Papers in Yiddish and East European Jewish Studies, 34 (New York: YIVO Institute for Jewish Research, 1979), B970.

4. Isaac Bashevis Singer, "Lezer shraybn" [Readers Write], *Forverts*, 9 Mar. 1957, p. 5; signed D. Segal.

5. Yitskhok Bashevis has been the only signature under which Singer's infrequent book reviews and literary essays had appeared in the *Tsukunft* during the late 1930's.

6. Isaac Bashevis Singer, "Der spinozist: Dertseylung" [The Spinozan: A Story], *Tsukunft*, 49, No. 7 (July 1944), 419–26; signed Yitskhok Bashevis. Trans. by Martha Glicklich and Cecil Hemley as "The Spinoza of Market Street," in *The Spinoza of Market Street* (New York: Farrar, Straus and Cudahy, 1961), pp. [3]–24.

7. Isaac Bashevis Singer, "Der kurtser fraytik" [Short Friday], *Tsukunft*, 50, No. 1 (Jan. 1945), 19–23; signed Yitskhok Bashevis. Tr. by Joseph Singer and Roger Klein as "Short Friday," in *Short Friday and Other Stories* (New York: Farrar, Straus and Giroux, 1964), pp. 228–43.

8. Isaac Bashevis Singer, "Gimpl tam" [Gimpl the Fool], *Yidisher kemfer*, 24, Whole no. 593 (30 Mar. 1945), 17–20; signed Yitskhok Bashevis. Tr. by Saul Bellow as "Gimpel the Fool," in *Gimpel the Fool and Other Stories* (New York: Noonday, 1957), pp. 3–21.

9. Isaac Bashevis Singer, "Di kleyne shusterlekh: Dertseylung" [The Little Shoemakers: A Story], *Tsukunft*, 50, No. 4 (April 1945), 232–41; signed Yitskhok Bashevis. Tr. by Isaac Rosenfeld as "The Little Shoemakers," in *Gimpel the Fool,* pp. [89]–119.

10. The first two to appear were Isaac Bashevis Singer, "Zaydlus der ershter: Fun a serye dertseylungen 'Dos gedenkbukh fun yeytser-hore'" [Zaydlus the First: From the Series of "Devil's Memoirs"], *Svive*, [OS], No. 1 (Jan.–Feb. 1943), pp. 11–24; and "Der roye veeyne-nire: Fun a serye dertseylungen 'Dos gedenkbukh fun yeytser-hore'" [Seer but Not Seen: From the Series of "Devil's Memoirs"], *Svive*, [OS], No. 4 (July–Aug. 1943), pp. 16–31; both signed Yitskhok Bashevis. These stories were translated, resp., by Joel Blocker and Elizabeth Pollet as "Zeidlus the

Pope," in *Short Friday*, pp. [176]–89; and by Norbert Guterman and Elaine Gottlieb as "The Unseen," in *Gimpel the Fool*, pp. 171–205. Other stories, clearly from the same series, appeared without subtitle; see Chone Shmeruk, "The Use of Monologue as a Narrative Technique in the Short Stories of Isaac Bashevis Singer," in *Der shpigl un andere dertseylungen* ([Tel Aviv]: Hebreisher universitet in Yerusholayim, Yidish-opteylung un Komitet far yidisher kultur in Yisroel, 1975), pp. xvi–xviii et passim.

11. See Singer's letter of 10 Aug. 1973, cited by Shmeruk, p. xiv, n. 18.

12. Isaac Bashevis Singer, "Der katlen: A bobe-mayse" [The Wife Killer: An Old Wive's Tale], *Yidisher kemfer*, 25, Whole no. 615 (7 Sept. 1945), 52–56; signed Yitskhok Bashevis. Cited After the unaltered rpt. in *Der shpigl*, pp. 54–74. Translations here – as throughout this chapter – are my own.

13. On fictive place names in the works of Singer's precursors, see David Neal Miller, "'Don't Force Me to Tell You the Ending: Closure in the Short Fiction of Sh. Rabinovitsh (Sholem-Aleykhem)," *Neophilologus*, 66, No. 1 (Jan. 1982), 110 (n. 14).

14. I.e., "[verbal] techniques for avoidance of evil"; see James A Matisoff, *Blessings, Curses, Hopes, and Fears: Psycho-Ostensive Expressions in Yiddish* (Philadelphia: Institute for the Study of Human Issues, 1979), Ch. 7 ("Malo-Fugition: Deliver Us From Evil!"), pp. 34–54.

15. On the history of the *ets-enk* conjugation, see Maks Vaynraykh (Max Weinreich), *Geshikhte fun der yidisher shprakh* (New York: YIVO Institute for Jewish Research, 1973), II, par. 124 (Bayerish-estraykhishn in determinant daytsh), 103: "Haynt zaynen zey simonim fun tsentral-yidish, nor amolike tsaytn . . . hob zey gekert greykhn vayter" [Today they are signs of Central Yiddish, but at one time they likely extended further]; see also IV, 142. A study of *ets-enk* from a sociolinguistic perspective remains a desideratum.

16. See Barbara Kirshenblatt-Gimblett, "Traditional Storytelling in the Toronto Jewish Community: A Study in the Performance and Creativity of an Immigrant Culture," Diss. Indiana 1972, esp. Ch. 8 ("Case Study of One Narrator and One Narrator Performance"), pp. 441–75. That the *bobe-mayse* is perceived of as a stable, named genre, and not merely an epithetic disparagement of the tale or its teller is confirmed by Barbara Myerhoff, *Number Our Days* (New York: Dutton, 1978), pp. 20, 31, 37, et passim.

17. Isaac Bashevis Singer, "Der shpigl: A monolog fun a shed" [The Mirror: A Monologue by a Demon], *Di goldene keyt*, Whole no. 26 (1956),

131–38; signed Yitskhok Bashevis; rpt. *Der shpigl,* pp. 1–11. Tr. by Norbert Guterman as "The Mirror," in *Gimpel the Fool,* pp. 77–88.

18. Isaac Bashevis Singer, "Dos fayer" [The Fire], *Forverts,* 25 Mar. 1956; signed Yitskhok Bashevis; rpt. *Der shpigl,* pp. 48–56. Tr. by Norbert Guterman as "Fire," in *Gimpel the Fool,* pp. 161–70. Citations are from *Der shpigl.*

19. Isaac Bashevis Singer, "Der tsurikgeshrigener" [The Man Who Was Called Back], *Forverts,* 24 Mar. 1957, sec. 2, p. 4; sec. 1, p. 6; signed Yitskhok Bashevis. Cited after the unaltered rpt. in *Gimpl tam un andere dertseylungen* (New York: Tsiko, 1963), pp. 51–61.

20. See Barbara Kirshenblatt-Gimblett, pp. 468–71.

21. Isaac Bashevis Singer, *Mayn tatns bezdn-shtub* [My Father's Rabbinical Court], *Forverts,* 19 Feb.–30 Sept. 1955; signed Yitskhok Varshavski. Rpt. (rev.; New York: Kval, 1956); signed Yitskhok Bashevis. Singer stated in a seminar at the State University of New York at Albany on 4 Sept. 1980 that he had requested the book-length collection also be signed Yitskohk Varshavski – a request declined by the publisher. Tr. by Channah Kleinerman-Goldstein, Elaine Gottlieb, and Joseph Singer as *In My Father's Court* (New York: Farrar, Straus and Giroux, 1966).

22. Isaac Bashevis Singer, *Der shrayberklub* [The Writers' Club], *Forverts,* 13 Jan.–29 Dec. 1956; signed Yitskhok Varshavski.

23. Singer's memoiristic writings merit more critical attention than they have thus far received. Edwin Gittleman's preliminary study of *Mayn tatns bezdn-shtub* is hampered by the author's access to the text only in a much-abridged English translation; "Isaac's Nominal Case: *In My Father's Court,*" in *Critical Views of Isaac Bashevis Singer,* ed. Irving Malin (New York: New York Univ. Press, 1969), pp. 194–206. Two excellent discussions of Singer's more recent autobiographical writings are Chone Shmeruk, "Bashevis Singer – in Search of His Autobiography," *Jewish Quarterly,* 29, No. 4 (Winter 1981–82), 28–36; and Anita Susan Grossman, unpublished review article on Singer's memoiristic trilogy, *A Little Boy in Search of God* (1976), *A Young Man in Search of Love* (1978), and *Lost in America* (1981).

24. Isaac Bashevis Singer, "Di mume Yentl" [Aunt Yentl], in *Mayn tatns bezdn-shtub,* pp. [331]–35.

25. Isaac Bashevis Singer, "Bilgoray," in *Mayn tatns bezdn-shtub,* pp. 320–24; the quoted passage is from pp. 323–24.

26. A collation of these pieces as they appear in successive versions is a major bibliographical desideratum. Four pieces not included

in the English translated edn. are collected in *An Isaac Bashevis Singer Reader* (New York: Farrar, Straus and Giroux, 1971), pp. [285]–313.

27. See my discussion of "What Women Know: Traditional Narration in Isaac Bashevis Singer's 'Big and Little,'" forthcoming in *Tradition and Transformation: Women in Jewish Culture,* ed. Gila Ramras-Rauch et al.

28. Isaac Bashevis Singer, "Author's Note," in *In My Father's Court,* tr. Channah Kleinerman-Goldstein, Elaine Gottlieb, and Joseph Singer (New York: Farrar, Straus and giroux, 1966), p. vii. This note is not present in any of the Yiddish edns.

29. Isaac Bashevis Singer, "Tsaytl un Rikl" [Tsaytl and Rikl], *Forverts,* 19 and 20 Aug. 1966; rpt. in *Der shpigl,* pp. 88–100; "Di nodl" [The Needle], *Kheshbn,* Whole no. 44 (1966), pp. 15–21; both signed Yitskhok Bashevis. Cone Shmeruk discusses an earlier version of 'Di nodle" not framed as first-person narrative; "The Use of Monologue as a Narrative Technique in the Stories of Isaac Bashevis Singer," in *Der shpigl,* pp. xxii–xxv.

30. Isaac Bashevis Singer, "Bendit un Dishke: Der mume Yentls a monolog" [Bendit and Dishke: A Monologue by Mume Yentl], *Tsukunft,* No. 3 (Mar. 1973), pp. 133–39; signed Yitskhok Bashevis; rpt. *Der shpigl,* pp. 121–35. In a letter to Chone Shmeruk dated 10 Aug. 1973, Singer writes "Di dertseylung 'Bendit un Dishke . . . iz hipshe etlekhe yor gelegn bay mir in a shuflod, ober nisht lenger vi velkhe 6 oder 7 yor" [The story "Bendit and Dishke" lay in a drawer a good many years, but no longer than some six or seven years]; see *Der shpigl,* p. xv. n. 19.

31. Curiously, L[eonard] P[rager]'s excellent article on Singer in the *Encyclopedia Judaica* is alphabetized under the letter *B* – an example of the extent to which a fictional persona has usurped the role of the historical author; "Isaac Bashevis Singer," in *Encyclopedia Judaica,* IVB (Jerusalem: Keter, 1972), col. 294.

32. Isaac Bashevis Singer, "Oyf der potshine" [On the Sidewalk], *Forverts,* 17 and 18 Sept. 1965; signed Yitskhok Bashevis; rpt. in *Der shpigl,* pp. 75–87.

33. Isaac Bashevis Singer, "Mendl bagreber" [Mendl the Gravedigger], *Forverts,* 20 and 21 Mar. 1970; signed Yitskhok Bashevis; rpt. in *Der shpigl,* pp. 111–20.

34. Isaac Bashevis Singer, "Not for the Sabbath," in *Old Love* (New York: Farrar, Straus and Giroux, 1979), pp. 169–81; tr. unacknowledged.

35. Isaac Bashevis Singer, "Der lantukh" [The *Lantukh*], *Di goldene keyt*, Whole no. 71 (1970), pp. 44–50; signed Yitskhok Bashevis. Tr. by the author and Laurie Colwin as "The Lantuch," in *A Crown of Feathers and Other Stories* (New York: Farrar, Straus and Giroux, 1973), pp. 92–101.

36. Isaac Bashevis Singer, "The Lantuch," in *Naftali the Story-teller and His Horse, Sus, and Other Stories* (New York: Farrar, Straus and Giroux, 1976); rpt. (New York: Dell, 1979), pp. [49]–58; tr. Joseph Singer. Citations are from the Dell edn. It is difficult to establish the dates of composition of Singer's children's stories with any degree of certitude since, as a rule, they appear only in English translation – often, as with "The Lantuch," only in collection. Since, however, the collection of texts for children immediately preceding *Nafali the Storyteller* was published in 1967, it is reasonable to assume a date of composition for "The Lantuch" of sometime between 1967 and 1975.

37. Regrettably, the translators chose to render these passages as indirect discourse, rather than narrated monologue (*erlebte Rede*).

38. See, for example, Isaac Bashevis Singer, "Der sod" [The Secret], in *Mayn tatns bezdn-shtub*, p. 80

39. Bruno Bettelheim discusses the supernatural in children's fiction from a reader-response point of view in *The Uses of Enchantment: The Meaning and Importance of Fairy Tales* (New York: Knopf, 1976).

40. Isaac Bashevis Singer, *Alone in the Wild Forest* (New York: Farrar, Straus and Giroux, 1971), tr. by the author and Elizabeth Shub. This book, published some six years prior to the publication of *Naftali the Storyteller*, is likely familiar to at least some of the child reader/auditors of "Growing Up," making them, too, participants in Singer's game of genre-mixing usually reserved for more mature readers.

41. Isaac Bashevis Singer, "A Day in Coney Island," in *A Crown of Feathers*, pp. 31–43; tr. by the author and Laurie Colwin; "The Psychic Journey," in *Old Love*, pp. 49–66; tr. by Joseph Singer; "Brother Beetle," in *Old Love*, pp. 123–33; tr. by the author and Elizabeth Shub.

42. Isaac Bashevis Singer, "Lost," in *A Crown of Feathers*, pp. 181–93; tr. by the author and Rosanna Gerber; "The Yearning Heifer," in *Passions*, pp. 88–103; tr. by the author and Ruth Schachner Finkel

43. Isaac Bashevis Singer, "The Admirer," in *Passions*, pp. 56–76; tr. by Joseph Singer.

44. Isaac Bashevis Singer, "One Night in Brazil," in *Old Love*, pp. 30; tr. by Joseph Singer.

45. Isaac Bashevis Singer, "The Briefcase," in *A Crown of Feathers*, pp. 110–34; tr. by Shulamith Charney; "There Are No Coincidences," *Old Love*, pp. 149–67; tr. not acknowledged.

46. Isaac Bashevis Singer, "The Briefcase," p. 110. Similarly, two stories in *A Crown of Feathers* have this Singer-like narrator living at different addresses in the same neighborhood – Riverside Drive ("The Egotist," p. 265) and Central Park West ("Neighbors," p. 309).

47. Isaac Bashevis Singer, *Der bal-tshuve* [The Penitent] (Tel Aviv: Y.-L. Perets, 1974). Tr. as *The Penitent* (New York: Farrar, Straus and Giroux, 1983).

48. Isaac Bashevis Singer, "Hanka: Dertseylung" [Hanka: A Story], *Di goldene keyt*, Whole no. 83 (1974), pp. 74–88; signed Yitskhok Bashevis. Tr. by the author and Blanche and Joseph Nevel as "Hanka," in *Passions*, pp. 3–23.

49. *Farshnitn*, lit. 'severed,' is a frequent Yiddish euphemism for "murdered." Cf. *A shpigl oyf a shteyn: Antologye, poezye un proze fun tsvelf farshnitene yidishe shraybers in Ratnfarband* [A Mirror on a Stone: Anthology of Poetry and Prose by Twelve Yiddish Writers Murdered in the Soviet Union], ed. Benjamin Hrushovski, Chone Shmeruk, and Avrom Sutskever (Tel Aviv: Farlag Di goldene keyt–Y.-L. Perets, 1964).

50. On the *kneytsh* in Perets' short fiction, see the "Introduction" by Irving Howe and Eliezer Greenberg to I. L. Peretz (i.e. Y.-L. Perets), *Selected Stories* (New York: Schocken, 1974), p. 18.

Chapter 4

1. Pedro Calderón de la Barca, *La vida es sueño*, 2:19:195–96 (Zaragoza: Editorial Ebro, 1959), p. 94. I am grateful to Marjorie Neidelman for having pointed out this early use of *ficción* [fiction] in an especially apt context.

2. Jackson R. Bryer and Paul E. Rockwell, "Isaac Bashevis Singer in English: A Bibliography," in *Critical Views of Isaac Bashevis Singer*, ed. Irving Malin (New York: New York Univ. Press, 1969) pp. 220–65.

3. Irving Buchen, *Isaac Bashevis Singer and the Eternal Past* (New York: New York Univ. Press, 1968), pp. 1–30 et passim.

4. Paul Kresh, *Isaac Bashevis Singer: The Magician of West 86th Street* (New York: Dial, 1979).

5. See, for example, Amy Sabrin's untitled article distributed by the *New York Times* Press Service and the Associated Press on 17 Oct. 1978.

6. Cited by Kresh, p. 345.

7. Richard Burgin, "Isaac Bashevis Singer Talks ... About Everything," *New York Times Magazine* (sec. 6), 26 November 1978, p. 24.

8. The substance and mechanics of Singer's correspondence are discussed by Hanna F. Desser, Dear Mr. Singer, Please send at once ...,'" *Present Tense*, 6, No. 2 (Winter 1979) 6-7.

9. Isaac Bashevis Singer, "What's in It for Me?" *Harper's*, 231 October 1965), 166-67.

10. Philip Roth, "Roth and Singer on Bruno Schulz," *New York Times Book Review* (sec. 7), 13 February 1977, pp. 5, 14, 16, 20.

11. Marshall Breger and Bob Barnhart, "A Conversation with Isaac Bashevis Singer," *The Handle* (Univ. of Pennsylvania) 2 (Fall 1964–Winter 1965); report in *Critical Views*, p. 42, to which I have referred.

12. Grace Farrell Lee, "Seeing and Blindness: A Conversation with Isaac Bashevis Singer," *Novel: A Forum on Fiction*, 9, No. 2 (Winter 1976), 152.

13. Reena Sara Ribalow, "A Visit to Isaac Bashevis Singer," *The Reconstructionist*, 30 (29 May 1964), 21.

14. Grace Farrell Lee, "Seeing and Blindness," p. 153.

15. Richard Burgin, "A Conversation with Isaac Bashevis Singer," *Michigan Quarterly Review*, 17, No. 2 (Spring 1978), 17; Burgin's elipses.

16. Unsigned addendum to Paul Gray, "Singer's Song of the Polish Past," *Time* (3 July 1978), p. 82.

17. David M. Andersen, "Isaac Bashevis Singer: Conversations in California," *Modern Fiction Studies*, 16, No. 4 (Winter 1970-71), 424.

18. B. Midwood, "Short Visits with Five Writers and One Friend," *Esquire*, 74 (November 1970), 150-53.

19. David Neal Miller, "The *yunge*: The Education of a Readership," paper presented at the International Conference on Research on Yiddish Language and Literature (Oxford), August 1979.

20. See n. 7.

21. Dick Adler, "The Magician of 86th Street," *Book World* (Washington, DC) 29 October 1967, p. 8; Hugh Nissenson, "Singer: His Demons Are Real," *Vogue*, 169, No. 4 (April 1979), pp. 277, 313; Cathy Lynn Grossman, "The Story of Isaac," *Tropic* (Miami), 25 May 1980, pp. 10–12, 24–25, 28–31.

22. Grace Farrell Lee, "Stewed Prunes and Rice Pudding: College Students Eat and Talk with Isaac Bashevis Singer," *Contemporary Literature*, 19, No. 4 (Autumn 1978), 446–58; Cathy Lynn Grossman, "The Story of Isaac," see n. 21.

23. John M. Ellis, *the Theory of Literature: A Logical Analysis* (Berkeley: Univ. of California Press, 1974), p. 44; Ellis' italics.

24. Richard Burgin, "Isaac Bashevis Singer Talks . . . About Everything," p. 24.

25. Ralph L. Woods, comp., *The Joy of Jewish Humor* (New York: Essandes, 1969).

26. Israel Shenker, "Isaac Bashevis Singer's Perspective on God and Man," *New York Times*, 23 October 1968, p. 49.

27. Cited by Kresh, p. 352.

28. Richard Burgin, "From Conversations with Isaac Bashevis Singer," *Hudson Review*, 31, No. 4 (Winter 1978–79), 622.

29. David M. Andersen, "Isaac Bashevis Singer: Conversations in California," p. 433.

30. Morton A. Reichek, "Storyteller," *New York Times Magazine* (section 6), 23 March 1975, p. 24.

31. W. K. Wimsatt, Jr. and Monroe C. Beardsley, "The Intentional Fallacy," in *The Verbal Icon: Studies in the Meaning of Poetry*, ed. W. K. Wimsatt, Jr. (1954; rpt. New York: Noonday, 1966), p. 3.

32. Richard Burgin, "A Conversation with Isaac Bashevis Singer," p. 131.

33. David M. Andersen, Isaac Bashevis Singer: Conversations in California," p. 424.

34. Joseph McLellan, "Issac B. Singer After the Nobel," *Washington Post*, 14 October 1978, p. 81.

35. Laurie Colwin, "Isaac Bashevis Singer, Storyteller," *New York Times Book Review* (sec. 7), 23 July 1978, p. 23.

36. Herbert R. Lottman, "I. B. Singer, Storyteller," *New York Times Book Review* (sec. 7), 25 June 1972, pp. 32–33; Richard Burgin, "Isaac Bashevis Singer Talks . . . About Everything," p. 52; Laurie Colwin, "Isaac Bashevis Singer, Storyteller," p. 23.

37. Isaac Bashevis Singer, "Why I Write for Children," in *Nobel Lecture* (New York: Farrar, Straus and Giroux, 1979), pp. 13–14.

38. Sanford Pinsker, "Isaac Bashevis Singer: An Interview," *Critique: Studies in Modern Fiction,* 11, No. 2 (1969), 22.

39. Richard Burgin, "A Conversation with Isaac Bashevis Singer," p. 123.

40. Morton A. Reichek, "Storyteller," p. 17.

41. Richard Burgin, "A Conversation with Isaac Bashevis Singer," p. 121.

42. Sander L. Gilman, "Interview/Isaac Bashevis Singer," *Diacritics,* 4, No. 1 (1974), 33.

43. Richard Burgin, "Isaac Bashevis Singer Talks . . . About Everything," p. 26.

44. Cathy Lynn Grossman, "The Story of Isaac," p. 24.

45. Philip Roth, "Roth and Singer on Bruno Schulz," p. 20.

46. Barbara Herrnstein Smith, "On the Margins of Discourse," *Critical Inquiry,* 1, No. 4 (June 1975), 773 et passim; cf. also her "Poetry as Fiction," *New Literary History,* 2, No. 2 (Winter 1971), 259–81.

47. Joel Blocker and Richard Elman, "An Interview with Isaac Bashevis Singer," *Commentary,* 36 (Nov. 1963); reported in *Critical Views,* p. 16, to which I have referred.

48. Buchen writes, "I have spent many hours talking and listening to Singer. . . . Wherever Singer's comments appear in this study and do not carry a specific reference to a published work, they are remarks garnered in actual conversation," *Isaac Bashevis Singer and the Eternal Past,* p. xiv, n. 3.

49. Buchen, pp. 20–21.

50. In the publisher's note to *Der sotn in Goray: A mayse fun fartsaytns, un andere dertseylungen* [Satan in Goray: A tale of Bygone Days, and Other Stories] (New York: Farlag Matones, 1943), we read: "Fun di finf dertseylungen, vos geyen arayn in dem bukh, iz nor eyne, 'Der

yid fun Bovl,' geshribn gevorn in Poyln. Di iberike fir zenen geshribn gevorn in Amerike, in 1942" [Of the five stories included in this book, only one, "The Jew from Babylon," was written in Poland. The remaining four were written in America in 1942] (p. [3]). This book, it should be noted, was published during the period of Singer's ostensible inactivity.

51. Richard Burgin, "Isaac Bashevis Singer Talks . . . About Everything," p. 26; Burgin's punctuation.

52. There were, to be fair, two pauses in Singer's production; 1934 – the year *before* his emigration to the United States – and mid-1937 to mid-1938. For details, see my *Bibliography of Isaac Bashevis Singer, 1924*-1949 (Berne: Peter Lang, 1983).

53. Sander L. Gilman, "Interview/Isaac Bashevis Singer," p. 33.

54. Paul Rosenblatt and Gene Koppel, *A Certain Bridge: Isaac Bashevis Singer on Literature and Life* (Tucson: Univ. of Arizona Press, 1971); rpt. as *Isaac Bashevis Singer on Literature and Life* (1979), p. 9.

Chapter 5

1. J. A. Eisenberg, "Isaac Bashevis Singer: Passionate Primitive or Pious Puritan?" in *Critical Views of Isaac Bashevis Singer*, ed. Irving Malin (New York: New York Univ. Press, 1969), pp. 48–67.

2. Laurie Colwin, "Isaac Bashevis Singer, Storyteller," *New York Times book Review* (sec. 7), 23 July 1978, p. 23; Herbert R. Lottman, "I. B. Singer, Storyteller," *New York Times Book Review* (sec. 7), 25 June 1972, pp. 32–33; Morton A. Reichek, "Storyteller," *New York Times Magazine* (sec. 6), 23 March 1975, p. 24.

3. Dick Adler, "The Magician of 86th Street," *Book World* (Washington, DC), 29 Oct. 1967, p. 8; Paul Kresh, *Isaac Bashevis Singer: The Magician of West 86th Street* (New York: Dial, 1979).

4. Isaac Bashevis Singer, "Why I Write for Children," in *Nobel Lecture* (New York: Farrar, Straus and Giroux, 1979), pp. 13–14.

Bibliography

Works by Isaac Bashevis Singer

Alone in the Wild Forest. New York: Farrar, Straus and Giroux, 1971. Tr. by the author and Elizabeth Shub.

"The Admirer." In *Passions* (q.v.), pp. 56–76. Tr. by Joseph Singer.

"Bendit un Dishke: Der mume Yentls a monolog" [Bendit and Dishke: A Monologue by Aunt Yentl] *Tsukunft*, No. 3 (March 1973), pp. 133–39. Signed Yitskhok Bashevis.

"The Briefcase." In *A Crown of Feathers* (q.v.), pp. 110–33. Tr. by the author and Laurie Colwin.

Der bal-tshuve [The Penitent]. Tel Aviv: Y.-L. Perets, 1974.

"Babske refues inem yidishn lebn fun amol" [Old Wives' Cures Among Jews of Yesterday]. *Forverts*, 12 July 1942, sec. 2, p. 2. Signed Yitskhok Varshavski.

A Crown of Feathers and Other Stories. New York: Farrar, Straus and Giroux, 1973.

"A Day in Coney Island." In *A Crown of Feathers* (q.v.), pp. 31–43. Tr. by the author and Laurie Colwin.

"Er hot a milyon dolar, ober er veyst nit vos m'tut mit zey" [He Has a Million Dollars He Doesn't Know What to Do With]. *Forverts*, 21 March 1946, p. 5. Signed D. Segal.

"Er gloybt in zayn vayb khotsh ale faktn zayen kegn ir" [Believes in His Wife Even Though Facts Are Stacked Against Her]. *Forverts*, 19 Jan. 1945, p. 5. Signed D. Segal.

"Er hot zikh geget mit zayn froy un zi genumen far [a] gelibter" [Divorced His Wife and Took Her as Lover]. *Forverts*, 21 May 1945, p. 5. Signed D. Segal.

"Er hot forgeshtelt zayn gelibte als zayn shvester" [He Introduced His Lover as His Sister]. *Forverts*, 26 Jan. 1945, p. 5. Signed D. Segal.

"Eyniklekh" [Grandchildren]. *Varshever shriftn*. Warsaw: Literatn-klub baym fareyn fun yidishe literatn un zhurnalistn in Varshe, 1926–27. Fourth sequence, pp. 2–11. Signed Yitskhok Bashevis.

"Dos fayer" [The Fire]. *Forverts*, 25 March 1956; rpt. in *Der shpigl* (q.v.), pp. 48–56. Signed Yitskhok Bashevis. Tr. by Norbert Guterman as "Fire." In *Gimpel the Fool* (q.v.), pp. 161–70.

"Fragn tsu undzere lezer vegn purim un peysekh" [We Ask Our Readers About Purim and Passover]. *Forverts*, 15 Dec. 1946, p. 2. Signed Yitskhok Varshavski.

"A froy hot fartroyt dem redaktor a vikhtikn sod" [Woman Trusts Editor with Important Secret.] *Forverts*, 15 Dec. 1947, p. 5. Signed D. Segal.

"Geburt-kontrol – A frage nit bloyz farn privatn lebn nor oykh far der politik fun felker un regirungen" [Birth Control: More than a Private Matter – One That Touches the Politics of States and Peoples]. *Forverts*, 14 Feb. 1943, p. 3. Signed Yitskhok Varshavski.

"Getsl malpe" [Getsl the Monkey]. In *Mayses fun hintern oyvn* (q.v.), pp. 165–76. Signed Yitskhok Bashevis. Tr. by the author and Ellen Kantarov as "Getzel the Monkey." In *The Seance* (q.v.), pp. 135–43.

Gimpel the Fool and Other Stories. New York: Noonday, 1957.

"Gimpl tam" [Gimpl the Fool]. *Yidisher kemfer*, 24, Whole no. 593 (30 March 1945), 17–20. signed Yitskhok Bashevis. Tr. by Saul Bellow as "Gimpel the Fool," in *Gimpel the Fool* (q.v.) pp. 3–21.

"Hanka: Dertseylung" [Hanka: A Story]. *Di goldene keyt*, Whole no. 83 (1974), pp. 74–88. Signed Yitskhok Bashevis. Tr. by the author and Blanche and Joseph Nevel as "Hanka." In *Passions* (q.v.), pp. 3–23.

"Der heldisher kamf fun yidn kegn di natsis in der varshever geto" [Heroic Battle of Jews Against Nazis in the Warsaw Ghetto]. *Forverts*, 4 July 1943, pp. 2, 4. Signed Yitskhok Varshavski.

"Hene fayer" [Hene Fire]. In *Mayses fun hintern oyvn* (q.v.), pp. 165–76. Signed Yitskhok Bashevis. Tr. by the author and Dorothea Straus as "Henne Fire." In *The Seance* (q.v.), pp. 123–34.

"Hitlers geshray az er firt milkhomes kegn yidn" [Hitler's Battle Cry Against the Jews]. *Forverts*, 7 Aug. 1944, pp. 2, 3. Signed Yitskhok Varshavski.

"In a leydiker shtub: Dertseylun" [In an Empty Home: A Story]. *Forverts*, 11 April 1937, p. 3. Signed Yitskhok Bashevis.

In My Father's Court. New York: Farrar, Straus and Giroux, 1966. Tr. by Channah Kleinerman-Goldstein, Elaine Gottlieb, and Joseph Singer.

"An interesante debate: Hot Hitler vild gemakht Daytshland oder der 'daytsher gayst' hot geshafn Hitlern?" [An Interesting Controversy: Did Hitler Uncivilize Germany or Did the German Spirit Create Hitler?]. *Forverts*, 10 Jan. 1943, p. 3. Signed Yitskhok Varshavski.

"Ir khosn hot zikh farlibt in ir mame" [Her Fiancé Fell in Love with Her Mother]. *Forverts*, 23 March 1945, p. 7. Signed D. Segal.

"Der kishef-makher" [The Conjuror]. *Forverts*, 21 May 1972. Signed Yitskhok Bashevis. Tr. by Joseph Singer as "The Sorcerer." In *Passions* (q.v.), pp. 244–55.

"Kleyn un groys" [Little and Big]. *Forverts*, 18 Oct. 1959. Rpt. in *Gimpl tam* (q.v.), pp. 248–55. Tr. by Mirra Ginsburg as "Big and Little." In *Short Friday* (q.v.), pp. [15]–25. Signed Yitskhok Bashevis.

"Di kleyne shusterlekh: Dertseylung" [The Little Shoemakers: A Story]. *Tsukunft*, 50, No. 4 (April 1945), 232.41. Signed Yitskhok Bashevis. Tr. by Isaac Rosenfeld as "The Little Shoemakers." In *Gimpel the Fool* (q.v.), pp. [89]–119.

Der kuntsnmakher fun Lublin [the Magician of Lublin]. 1958; rpt. Tel Aviv: Y.-L. Perets, 1971. Signed Yitskhok Bashevis. Tr. by Elaine Bottlieb and Joseph Singer as *The Magician of Lublin.* New York: Noonday, 1960.

"Der kurtser fraytik" [Short Friday]. *Tsukunft*, 50, No. 1 (Jan. 1945), 19–23. Signed Yitskhok Bashevis. Tr. by Joseph Singer and Roger Klein as "Short Friday." In *Short Friday* (q.v.), pp. 228–43.

"The Lantuch." In *Naftali the Storyteller* (q.v.), pp. [49]–58. Tr. by Joseph Singer.

"Der lantukh" [The Lantukh]. *Di goldene keyt,* Whole no. 71 (1970), pp. 44–50. Signed Yitskhok Bashevis. Tr. by the author and Laurie Colwin as "The Lantuch." In *A Crown of Feathers* (q.v.), pp. 92–101.

"Lezer fun *Forverts* gibn eytses a yidn vegn vi oystsugebn a milyon dolor" [*Forward* Readers Advise How to Spend a Million Dollars]. *Forverts,* 17 Feb. 1947, p. 5. Signed D. Segal.

"Lezer fun *Forverts* zogn zikh aroys vegn a vikhtiker frage" [*Forverts* Readers Speak Out on Crucial Issue]. *Forverts,* 22 Dec. 1947, p. 5. Signed D. Segal.

"Lezer shraybn" [Readers Write]. *Forverts,* 9 March 1957, p. 5. Signed D. Segal.

"A litvisher yid, velkher iz geven a betler, a kemfer far emes un eyner fun di greste filozofn in der velt" [A Lithuanian Jew Who Was a Beggar, Fighter for the Truth, and One of the World's Great Philosophers]. *Forverts,* 16 April 1939, sec. 2, p. 3; 23 April 1939, sec. 2, p. 3. Signed Yitskhok Varshavski.

"Lost." In *A Crown of Feathers* (q.v.), pp. 181–93. Tr. by the author and Rosanna Gerber.

Lost in America. Garden City, NY: Doubleday, 1981.

"Mames, shvigers, shvester un brider, vos makhn a beyz lebn tsvishn man un vayb" [Mothers, Mothers-in-Law, Sisters and Brothers Who Promote Trouble Between Husband and Wife]. *Forverts,* 14 April 1940, sec. 2, pp. 2, 4. Signed Yitskhok Varshavski.

"Mayn tatns bezdn-shtub" [My Father's Rabbinical Court]. *Forverts,* 19 Feb.–30 Sept. 1955. Signed Yitskhok Varshavski. Rpt. (rev.) as *Mayn tatns bezdn-shtub.* New York: Kval, 1956. Signed Yitskhok Bashevis. Tr. by Channah Kleinerman-Goldstein, Elaine Gottlieb, and Joseph Singer as *In My Father's Court.* New York: Farrar, Straus and Giroux, 1966

Mayses fun hintern oyvn [Stories from Behind the Stove]. Tel Aviv: Y.-L. Perets, 1971.

Mazel and Shlimazel, or The Milk of a Lioness. New York: Farrar, Straus and Giroux, 1967. Tr. by Elizabeth Shub and the author.

"Mendl bagreber" [Mendl the Gravedigger]. *Forverts,* 20 and 21 March 1970; rpt. in *Der shpigl* (q.v.), pp. 111–20. Signed Yitskhok Bashevis.

"Mener vos vern oyf di eltere yorn romantish" [Men Who Turn Romantic in Old Age]. *Forverts,* 24 Sept. 1945, p. 2. Signed Yitskhok Varshavski.

"Mir viln nemen undzere lezer far shutfim" [We Want Our Readers as Partners]. *Forverts*, 24 Sept. 1945, p. 2. Signed Yitskhok Varshavski.

"Di mume Yentl" [Aunt Yentl]. In *Mayn tatns bezdn-shtub* (q.v.), pp. [331]–35. Signed Yitskhok Varshavski. Tr. as "Aunt Yentel." In *In My Father's Court* (q.v.), pp. 281–85.

Naftali the Storyteller and His Horse, Sus, and Other Stories. New York: Farrar, Straus and Giroux, 1976; rpt. New York: Dell, 1979.

"A naye grupe in der yidisher literatur? [A New Yiddish Literary Group?]. *Forverts*, 26 Dec. 1948, sec. 2, p. 5. Signed Yitskhok Varshavski.

"Nayes fun yidishn lebn in Palestine: Sovet-rusland vet zikh nit mishn in der frage fun emigratsye keyn Erets-yisroel" [News of Jewish Life in Palestine: Soviet Russia Won't Interfere with Jewish Emigration to Palestine]. *Forverts*, 26 Jan. 1945. Signed Yitskhok Varshavski.

"Nekhamy Vinavers muzikalish verk 'Der zibeter tog'" [Nekhamye Vinaver's Composition *The Seventh Day*]. *Forverts*, 13 Dec. 1946. Signed B. [sic] Segal.

"Di nodl" [The Needle]. *Kheshbn*, Whole no. 44 (1966) pp. 15–21. Signed Yitskhok Bashevis. Tr. by the author and Elizabeth Shub as "The Needle." In *The Seance* (q.v.), pp. 155–63.

"Not for the Sabbath." In *Old Love* (q.v.), pp. 169–81. Tr. unacknowledged.

Old Love. New York: Farrar, Straus, and Giroux, 1979.

"One Day in Brazil." In *Old Love* (q.v.), p. 3–20. Tr. by Joseph Singer.

"Oyf der potshine" [On the Sidewalk]. *Forverts*, 17 and 18 Sept. 1965; rpt. in *Der shpigl* (q.v.), pp. 75–87.

'Oyfn oylem-hatoye" [In the World of Chaos]. *Di yidishe velt: Khoydesh-shrift far literatur, kritik, kunst un kultur*, No. 1 (April 1928), pp. 53–64. Signed Yitskhok Bashevis.

Passions and Other Stories. New York: Farrar, Straus and Giroux, 1975.

"The Psychic Journey." In *Old Love* (q.v.), pp. 49–66. Tr. by Joseph Singer.

"Romanen un libes bay khayes, beheymes un feygl" [Love and Romance Among Birds and Beasts]. *Forverts*, 19 May 1940, sec. 2, pp. 2, 4. Signed Yitskhok Varshavski.

"Der roye veeyne-nire: Fun a serye dertseylungen 'Dos gedenkbukh fun yeytser-hore'" [Seer but Not Seen: From the Series of "Devil's Memoirs"[. *Svive*, [OS], No. 1 (Jan–Feb. 1943, pp. 11–24. Signed Yitskhok Bashevis. Tr. by Norbert Guterman and Elaine Gottlieb as "The Unseen." In *Gimpel the Fool* (q.v.), pp. 171–205.

"Sale: A bild" [Sale: A Portrait]. *Literarishe bleter,* 9, No. 1 (1 Jan. 1932), 7–8. Signed Yitskhok Bashevis.

"Sam Palka and David Vishkover." In *Passions* (q.v.), pp. 133–47. Tr. by the author and Dorothea Straus.

The Seance and Other Stories. New York: Farrar, Straus and Giroux, 1968.

Short Friday and Other Stories. New York: Farrar, Straus and Giroux, 1964.

"Der shpigl: A monolog fun a shed" [The Mirror: A Monologue by a Demon]. *Di goldene keyt,* Whole no. 26 (1956), 131–38; rpt. in *Der shpigl* (q.v.), pp. 1–11. Signed Yitskhok Bashevis.

Der Shpigl un andere dertseylungen [The Mirror and Other Stories]. Ed. Chone Shmeruk. [Tel Aviv]: Hebreisher universitet in Yerushalayim, Yidish-opteylung un Komitet far yidisher kultur in yisroel, 1975.

"Shteyner vos faln arop fun himl" [Rocks That Fall from the Skies]. *Forverts,* 12 Nov. 1944, pp. 4, 3. Signed Yitskhok Varshavski.

"Shvues–der yontev fun nemen di toyre" [Shavuous–The Holiday of Receiving the Torah]. *Forverts,* 6 June 1957, p. 2. Signed Yitskhok Varshavski.

Der sotn in Goray: A mayse fun fartsaytns [Satan in Goray: A Tale of Bygone Days]. 1933; collected Warsaw: Biblyotek fun yidishn p.e.n.-klub. 1935; rpt. (rev.) New York: Farlag Matones, 1943; rpt. Jerusalem: Hebreisher universitet, 1972. Tr. by Jacob Sloan as *Satan in Goray.* New York: Noonday, 1955.

The Spinoza of Market Street. New York: Farrar, Straus, and Cudahy, 1961.

"Der spinozist: Dertseylung" [The Spinozan: A Story]. *Tsukunft,* 49, No. 7 (July 1944), 419–26. Signed Yitskhok Bashevis. Tr. by Martha Glicklich and Cecil Hemley as "The Spinoza of Market Street." In *The Spinoza of Market Street* (q.v.), pp. [3]–24.

"Stsenes fun yomerlekhn dales in Varshe" [Scenes of Bitter Poverty in Warsaw]. *Forverts,* 6 Aug. 1944, sec. 2, p. 3. Signed Yitskhok Varshavski.

"There Are No Coincidences." In *Old Love* (q.v.), pp. 149–67. Tr. not acknowledged.

"Di tokhter hot zikh ayngeredt az zi an aktrise" [Daughter Persuades Herself She's an Actress]. *Forverts,* 11 May 1945, p. 5. Signed D. Segal.

"Tsaytl un Rikl" [Tsaytl and Rikl]. *Forverts,* 19 and 20 Aug. 1966; rpt. in *Der shpigl* (q.v.), pp. 88–100. Signed Yitskhok Bashevis. tr. by Mirra Ginsburg as "Zeitl and Rickel." In *The Seance* (q.v.), pp. 102–13.

"Tsu der frage fun dikhtung un politik" [Poetry and Politics], *Globus* [1], No. 3 (Sept. 1932), 39–49. Signed Yitskhok Bashevis.

"Der tsurikgeshrigener" [The Man Who Was Called Back]. *Forverts,* 24 March 1957, sec. 2, p. 4; sec. 1, p. 6. Signed Yitskhok Bashevis.. Tr. by Mirra Ginsburg as "The Man Who Came Back." in *The Spinoza of Market Street* (q.v.), pp. [122]–34.

"Tsurikvegs" [The Way Back]. *Literarishe bleter,* 5, No. 47 (23 Nov. 1928), 927. Signed Yitskhok Bashevis.

"A Tutor in the Village." In *Passions* (q.v.), pp. 148–61. Tr. by the author and Rosanna Gerber Cohen.

"Verter oder bilder" [Words or Pictures]. *Literarishe bleter,* 4, No. 34 (26 Aug. 1927), 663–65. Signed Yitskhok Bashevis.

"Vi azoy shvues iz gevorn der yontev fun der toyre" [How Shavuous Became the Holiday of the Torah]. *Forverts,* 3 June 1949, p. 2. Signed Yitskhok Varshavski.

"Vi eltern darfn handlen ven zeyer tokhter firt a libe mit a farheyratn man" [How Parents Should Act When Their Daughter Has an Affair with a Married Man]. *Forverts,* 18 Dec. 1947, pp. 2, 7. Signed Menakhem Podolyer.

"Vos es falt alts fun himl!" [The Things That Fall from the Skies!]. *Forverts,* 14 Feb. 1957, pp. 2, 3. Signed Yitskhok Varshavski.

"What's in It for Me?" *Harper's,* 231 (Oct. 1965), 166–67.

"Why I Write for Children." In *Nobel Lecture.* New York: Farrar, Straus and Giroux, 1979. Pp. 13–14.

"Der yid fun Bovl" [The Jew from Babylon]. *Globus* [1], No. 2 (July [i.e. Aug.] 1932), 17–27. Signed Yitskhok Bashevis.

"Di yidishe shprakh un kultur lebt iber ir greste krizis" [Yiddish Language and Culture Undergo Their Greatest Crisis]. *Forverts,* 4 Dec. 1944, pp. 4, 3. Signed Yitskhok Varshavski.

"A yidisher diktator in Drohobitsh, mit velkher s'hot gekokht gants Galitsye" [The Jewish Dictator of Drohobycz—The Rage of Galicia]. *Forverts,* 30 April 1939, p. 7; 7 May 1939, p. 5. Signed Yitskhok Varshavski.

"Yidn vos zaynen avek fun der heym un zikh gelozt zukhn glik" [Jews Who Made Off to Seek Their Fortune]. *Forverts*, 8 April 1947, pp. 2, 6. Signed A. [sic] Segal.

A Young Man in Search of Love. Garden City, N.Y.: Doubleday, 1978.

"A zokh: A khronik" [An Old Man: A Chronicle]. *Globus: Khoydesh-zhurnal far literatur*, [1], No. 3 (Sept. 1932), 39–49. Signed Yitskhok Bashevis.

Interviews with Isaac Bashevis Singer

Adler, Dick, "The Magician of 86th Street." *Book World* (Washington, D. C.), 29 Oct. 1967, p. 8.

Andersen, David M. "Isaac Bashevis Singer: Conversations in California." *Modern fiction Studies*, 16, No. 4 (Winter 1970–71), 424.

Blocker, Joel and Richard Elman. "An Interview with Isaac Bashevis Singer." *Commentary*, 36 (Nov. 1963); rpt. in *Critical Views of Isaac Bashevis Singer* (q.v.), pp. 3–26.

Breger, Marshall adn Bob Barnhart. "A Conversation with Isaac Bashevis Singer." *The Handle* (Univ. of Pennsylvania), 2 (Fall 1964–Winter 1965); rpt. in *Critical Views of Isaac Bashevis Singer* (q.v.), pp. 27–43.

Burgin, Richard. "A Conversation with Isaac Bashevis Singer." *Michigan Quarterly Review*, 17, No. 2 (Spring 1978) 17–23.

Burgin, Richard. "From conversations with Isaac Bashevis Singer." *Hudson review*, 31, No. 4 (Winter 1978–79), 622–24.

Burgin, Richard. "Isaac Bashevis Singer Talks . . . About Everything." *New York Times Magazine* (sec. 6), 26 Nov. 1978, p. 24.

Colwin, Laurie. "Isaac Bashevis Singer, Storyteller." *New York Times Book Review* (sec. 7), 23 july 1978, pp. 1, 23–24.

Gilman, Sander. "Interview/Isaac Bashevis Singer." *Diacritics*, 4, No. 1 (1974), 30–33.

Lee, Grace Farrell. "Seeing and Blindness: A Conversation with Isaac Bashevis Singer." *Novel: A Forum on Fiction*, 9, No. 2 (Winter 1976), 151–64.

Lee, Grace Farrell. "Stewed Prunes and Rice Pudding: College Students Eat and Talk with Isaac Bashevis Singer." *Contemporary Literature*, 19, No. 4 (Autumn 1978), 446–58.

Lottman, Herbert R. "I. B. Singer, Storyteller." *New York Times Book Review* (sec. 7), 25 June 1972, pp. 32–33.

McLellan, Joseph. "Isaac B. Singer After the Nobel." *Washington Post,* 14 Oct. 1978, p. 81.

Midwood, B. "Short Visits with Five Writers and One Friend." *Esquire,* 74 (Nov. 1970), 150–53.

Nissenson, Hugh. "Singer: His Demons Are Real." *Vogue,* 169 (April 1979), 277, 313.

Pinsker, Sanford. "Isaac Bashevis Singer: An Interview." *Critique: Studies in Modern Fiction,* 11, No. 2 (1969) 26–39.

Reichek, Morton A. "Storyteller." *New York Times Magazine* (sec. 6), 23 March 1975, pp. 16–18, 20, 22, 24, 26, 28, 30, 33.

Ribalow, Reena Sara. "A Visit to Isaac Bashevis Singer." *The Reconstructionist,* 30 (29 May 1964), 19–26.

Rosenblatt, Paul and Gene Koppel. *A Certain Bridge: Isaac Bashevis Singer on Literature and Life* (Tucson: Univ. of Arizona Press, 1971) rpt. as *Isaac Bashevis Singer on Literature and Life* (1979).

Roth, Philip. "Roth and Singer on Bruno Schulz." *New York Times Book Review* (sec. 7), 13 Feb. 1977, pp. 5, 14, 16, 20.

Shenker, Israel. "Isaac Singer's Perspective on God and Man." *New York Times,* 23 Oct. 1968, p. 49.

Works by Other Authors

The Achievement of Isaac Bashevis Singer. Ed. Marcia Allentuck. Carbondale: Southern Illinois Univ. Press, 1969.

Alexander, Edward. *Isaac Bashevis Singer.* TWAS 582 (Boston: Twayne, 1980).

Baumgarten, Murray. *City Scriptures: Modern Jewish Writing.* Cambridge, MA: Harvard Univ. Press, 1982.

Baumgarten, Murray. "The Historical Novel: Some Postulates." *Clio,* 4, No. 2 (Feb. 1975), 173–82.

Benjamin of Tudela. *The Itinerary of Benjamin of Tudela.* Ed. Nathan Adler. London, 1907; rpt. New York: Feldheim, n.d.

Bettelheim, Bruno. *The Uses of Enchantment; The Meaning and Importance of Fairy Tales.* New York: Knopf, 1976.

Bloom, Harold. "The Breaking of Form." In *Deconstruction and Criticism.* Ed. Harold Bloom, Paul de Man et al. New York: Seabury, 1979. Pp. 1–37.

Bryer, Jackson R. and Paul E. Rockwell. "Isaac Bashevis Singer in English: A Bibliography." In *Critical Views of Isaac Bashevis Singer* (q.v.), pp. 220–65.

Buchen, Irving. *Isaac Bashevis Singer adn the Eternal Past.* New York: New York Univ. Press, 1968.

Calderón de la Barca, Pedro. *La vida es sueño.* Zaragoza: Editorial Ebro, 1959.

Chametzky, Jules. *From the Ghetto: The Fiction of Abraham Cahan.* Amherst: Univ. of Massachusetts Press, 1972.

Critical Views of Isaac Bashevis Singer. Ed. Irving Malin. New York: New York Univ. Press, 1969.

D., A.-M. (=Ayzik-Meyer Dik?). *Malke veHadase* (etc.) Vilna: N. p., 1887.

Desser, Hanna F. "'Dear Mr. Singer, Please send at once . . .'" *Present Tense,* 6, No. 2 (Winter 1979), 6–7.

Dobroszycki, Lucjan and Barbara Kirshenblatt-Gimblett. *Image Before My Eyes: A Photographic History of Jewish Life in Poland, 1865–1939.* New York: Schocken, 1977.

Ellis, John M. *The Theory of Literary Criticism: A Logical Analysis.* Berkeley: Univ. of California Press, 1974.

Erlich, Victor. *Russian Formalism: History—Doctrine.* The Hague: Mouton, 1965.

Essays on Singer. Ed. David Neal Miller. [Under submission].

Filologishe shriftn fun Yivo. Warsaw, 1926–28.

Hawthorne, Nathaniel. Preface to *The Blithedale Romance.* Boston: Ticknor, Reed & Fields, 1852. Pp. iii–iv.

Hawthorne, Nathaniel. Preface to *The House of the Seven Gables: A Romance.* Boston: Ticknor, Reed & Fields, 1851. no pag.

Hawthorne, Nathaniel. Preface [15 Dec. 1859] to *The Marble Faun; or, the Romance of Monte Beni.* Boston: Ticknor and Fields, 1860.

Howe, Irving. *World of Our Fathers.* New York: Harcourt, 1976.

Kan, Ab. (Abraham Cahn). "Yankev Frank: Der firer fun der yidisher sekte (etc.)" [Yankev Frank: The Leader of the Jewish Sect. (etc.)]. *Forverts,* 5 oct. 1935, p. 12.

Kazin, Alfred. "Isaac Bashevis Singer and the Mind of God." in *Essays on Singer* (q.v.).

Kirshenblatt-Gimblett, Barbara. "The Concept and Varieties of Narrative Performance in East European Jewish Culture." In *Explorations in the Ethnicity of Speaking.* Ed. Richard Bauman and Joel Sherzer (Cambridge, Eng.: Cambridge Univ. Press, 1974). Pp 283–308.

Kirshenblatt-Gimblett, Barbara. "Traditional Storytelling in the Toronto Jewish Community: A Study in the Performance and Creativity in an Immigrant Culture." Diss. Indiana 1972.

Lardner, Ring. "*Clemo Uti* (The Water Lillies)." In *The Ring Lardner Reader.* Ed. Maxwell Geismar. New York: Scribner's, 1963. Pp. 599–601.

Leksikon fun der nayer yidisher literatur [Lexicon of Modern Yiddish Literature]. VII. New York: Alveltlekher yidisher kultur-kongres, 1968.

Lukács, Georg. *The Historical Novel* (1937). Tr. Hannah and Stanley Mitchell. London: Merlin, 1962.

Malin, Irving, *Isaac Bashevis Singer.* New York: Ungar, 1972.

Matisoff, James A. *Blessings, Curses, Hopes, and Fears: Psycho-Ostensive Expressions in Yiddish.* Philadelphia: Institute for the Study of Human Issues, 1979.

Miller, David Neal. *A Bibliography of Isaac Bashevis Singer, January 1950–June 1952.* Working Papers in Yiddish and East European Jewish Culture, 34. New York: YIVO Institute for Jewish Research, 1979.

Miller, David Neal. "'A Guest in the Editorial Offices': Singer's Pseudonymous Journalistic Fiction." Paper presented at the annual meeting of the Modern Language Assn. of America, 30 Dec. 1979.

Miller, David Neal. "The *yunge*: The Education of a Readership." Paper presented at the International Conference on Research in Yiddish Language and Literature (Oxford), 10 Aug. 1979.

Myerhoff, Barbara. *Number Our Days.* New York: Dutton, 1978.

Neugroschel, Joachim. "The Rabbi Who was Turned into a Werewolf." In *Yenne Velt: The Great Works of Jewish Fantasy and Occult*. Ed. Joachim Neugroschel. 1976; rpt. New York: Pocket Books, 1978. Pp. 31–43.

Opotshinski, Perets. *Reportazhn fun varshever geto*[*Reportazhn* from the Warsaw Ghetto]. Warsaw: Yidbukh, 1954.

Opotshinski, Perets. *Gezamlte shriftn* [Collected Writings]. New York: privately printed, 1951.

Peretz, I. L. (i.e. Y.–L. Perets). *Selected Stories*. Ed. Irving Howe and Eliezer Greenberg. New York: Schocken, 1974.

Peskof, Meyer. "Der militerisher shnayder Bornshteyn, velkher hot geshikt zayne finf zin in milkhome" [Bornstein, Tailor to the Military, Who Sent His Five Sons to War]. *Forverts*, 21 March 1946, p. 5.

P[rager], L[eonard]. "Isaac Bashevis Singer." In *Encyclopedia Judaica*. IVB. Jerusalem: Keter, 1972. col. 294.

Rabinovitsh, Sholem (Sholom Aleichem). "Kapores" [Scapegoats] (1903). In *Ale verk*. New York: Folksfond, 1918. VIII, [113]–26.

Rabinovitsh, Sholem (Sholom Aleichem). "Dos porfolk" [The Couple] (1909). In *Ale verk*. New York: Folksfond, 1918. VII, [127]–53. Tr. by Shlomo Katz as "The Pair." in *A Treasury of Yiddish Stories*. Ed. Irving Howe and Eliezer Greenberg. 1954; rpt. New York: Schocken, 1973. Pp. 192–205.

Rohrberger, Mary. *Hawthorne and the Modern Short Story*. The Hague: Mouton, 1966.

Roskies, David G. "The Medium and the Message of the Maskilic Chapbook." *Jewish Social Studies*, 41, Nos. 3–4 (Summer–Fall 1979), 275–90.

R[oth], C[ecil]. "Benjamin of Tudela." In *Encyclopedia Judaica*. IV. Jerusalem: Keter, 1972. Cols. 535–38.

Sabrin, Amy. Untitled article distributed by the *New York Times* Press Service and the Associated Press, 17 Oct. 1978.

Schaechter, Mordkhe. "The 'Hidden Standard': A Study of Competing Influences in Standardization." In *The Field of Yiddish: Studies in Language, Folklore, and Literature*. The Hague: Mouton, 1969. III, 284–304.

Shapiro, Lamed. "Der rov un di rebetsn" [The Rabbi and the Rabbi's Wife]. In *Di yidishe melukhe un andere zakhn.*. New York: Yidish lebn, 1929. Pp. [283]–85. Tr. Curt Leviant as "The Rabbi and the Rebbetsin." In *The Jewish Government and Other Stories*. Ed. Curt Leviant. New York: Twayne, 1971. Pp. 51–53.

Shaykevitsh, Nokhem-Meyer (pseud. Shomer). *Der baron un di markize: A hekhst-interestanter roman* [Der Baron and the Marchioness: A Highly Interesting Novel]. Odessa: Bletnitski, 1902.

Shaykevitsh, Nokhem-Meyer. *Di geheyme yidn: A roman fun der geshikhte in Shpanyen* [The Secret Jews: A Novel About Jewish History in Spain]. New York: Hebrew Publishing Co., n.d.

Shmeruk, Chone. "Bashevis Singer – in Search of His Autobiography." *Jewish Quarterly*, 29, No. 4 (Winter 1981–82), 28–36.

Shriftn fun der katedre far yidisher kultur ba der alukrainisher visnshaftlekher akademye – literarishe un filologishe sektsyes.. Kiev: Kultur-lige, 1928 ff.

Siegel, Ben. *Isaac Bashevis Singer*. Minneapolis: Univ. of Minnesota Press, 1969.

Slotnick, Susan A. "Isaac Bashevis Singer and the Yiddish Family Saga." In *Essays on Singer* (q.v.).

Vaynraykh, Maks (Max Weinreich). "Daytshmerish toyg nit" [*Daytshmerish* Is Wrong]. *Yidish far ale* (Vilna), 1 (1938), 97–106.

Weinreich, Uriel. *Modern English-Yiddish Yiddish-English Dictionary*. New York: McGraw-Hill, 1968.

Wiener, Leo. *The History of Yiddish Literature in the Nineteenth Century*. 1899; rpt. New York: Hermon, 1972.

Wimsatt, W. K., Jr., and Monroe C. Beardsley. "The Intentional Fallacy." In *The Verbal Icon: Studies in the Meaning of Poetry*. Ed. W. K. Wimsatt, Jr. 1954; rpt. New york: Noonday, 1966. Pp. 3–18.

Wolitz, Seth L. "The Two 'Yordim': I. B. Singer's Debt to Dovid Bergelson." In *Essays on Singer* (q.v.).

Woolf, Virginia. "The Shooting Party." *Harper's Bazaar* (London), March 1938, pp. 72, 100, 102. Rpt. (rev.) in *A Haunted House*. 1944; rpt. London: Hogarth, 1967. Pp. 59–68.

Zavarzadeh, Mas'ud. *The Mythopoeic Reality: The Postwar American Nonfiction Novel*. Urbana: Univ. of Illinois Press, 1976.

Index